LEWIS CARROLL
and his world

JOHN PUDNEY

LEWIS CARROLL

and his world

CHARLES SCRIBNER'S SONS

NEW YORK

Frontispiece: Lewis Carroll holding
a photographic lens. Taken in 1863
by O. G. Rejlander.

1   3   5   7   9   11   13   15   17   19   I/C   20   18   16   14   12   10   8   6   4   2

Printed in Great Britain
Library of Congress Catalog Card Number 76-7185

ISBN 0-684-14728-9

A THIRTY-YEAR-OLD Oxford mathematics don, the Revd Charles Lutwidge Dodgson, laid aside his white flannels and straw boater to assume his customary clerical gear, and wrote in the diary he meticulously kept: 'Duckworth and I made an expedition *up* the river to Godstow with the three Liddells: we had tea on the bank there, and did not reach Christ Church again till quarter past eight, when we took them on to my rooms to see my collection of micro-photographs, and restored them to the Deanery just before nine.' The date was 4 July 1862.

What the diarist did not mention at the time, but recorded later, was that one of the children, named Alice, had said, 'Tell us a story please.' Duckworth remembered this little girl saying, before leaving that evening, 'Oh, Mr Dodgson, I wish you would write out Alice's adventures for me.'

This could have been a long forgotten Victorian incident were it not that the tall, shy, child-doting bachelor called Dodgson had the

Alice, Lorina, Harry and Edith Liddell, children of the dean of Christ Church, photographed by Carroll *c.* 1858. It was for their entertainment that *Wonderland* was invented.

Lewis Carroll aged twenty-five, at the start of his career as a mathematics don at Christ Church.

pen-name Lewis Carroll, and that he carried out the wish of the little girl called Alice Liddell and wrote *Alice in Wonderland*.

The following day at the Great Western Railway station at Oxford he met Alice again with her family – waiting for the 9.2 morning train to London. Evidently he travelled separately: for before he reached Paddington he had the 'headings written out' for the story which first appeared as *Alice's Adventures Under Ground*.

Eight months later, in February 1863, he turned back to his diary entry and wrote on the opposite page that the 'fairy-tale . . . which I undertook to write out for Alice . . . is now finished (as to the text) though the pictures are not yet nearly done.'

Twenty-five years later he turned the scene into a fairy-tale in its own right:

I had sent my heroine straight down a rabbit-hole, to begin with, without the least idea what was to happen afterwards. . . . In writing it out, I added many fresh ideas, which seemed to grow of themselves upon the original stock; and many more added themselves when, years afterwards, I wrote it all over again for publication.

Full many a year has slipped away, since that 'golden afternoon' that gave thee birth, but I can call it up almost as clearly as if it were yesterday – the cloudless blue above, the watery mirror below, the boat drifting idly on its way, the tinkle of the drops that fell from the oars, as they waved so sleepily to and fro, and (the one bright gleam of life in all the slumberous scene) the three eager faces, hungry for news of fairy-land, and who would not be said 'nay' to: from whose lips 'Tell us a story, please' had all the stern immutability of Fate!

That golden afternoon! He had romanticized it from the outset. His introductory verses to the book started like this:

> All in the golden afternoon
>   Full leisurely we glide;
> For both our oars, with little skill,
>   By little arms are plied,
> While little hands make vain pretence
>   Our wanderings to guide.

And concluded with these lines:

> Thus grew the tale of Wonderland:
>   Thus slowly, one by one,
> Its quaint events were hammered out –
>   And now the tale is done,
> And home we steer, a merry crew,
>   Beneath the setting sun.

Was the Golden Afternoon in fact hallucinatory, an ecstatic memory which infected them all? In this century the Lewis Carroll cult has turned every conceivable stone with veneration, curiosity, scepticism, pedantry, and a certain measure of lunacy. So it is not surprising that a Carrollian sleuth went to the Meteorological Office and turned up the record showing that the afternoon was in fact 'cool and rather wet' at Oxford. In the twenty-four hours from 10 a.m. on 4 July 1862, 0.17 of an inch of rain fell, most of it after 2 p.m. and before 2 a.m. of 5 July.

Yet Canon (as he became) Robinson Duckworth recalled a 'beautiful summer afternoon'. Alice, more than thirty years after the event, stated: 'Nearly all of *Alice's Adventures Under Ground* was told on that blazing summer afternoon with the heat haze shimmering over the meadows where the party landed to shelter for a while in the shadow cast by the haycocks near Godstow.'

of her own little sister. So the boat wound slowly along, beneath the bright summer-day, with its merry crew and its music of voices and laughter, till it passed round one of the many turnings of the stream, and she saw it no more.

Then she thought, (in a dream within the dream, as it were,) how this same little Alice would, in the after-time, be herself a grown woman: and how she would keep, through her riper years, the simple and loving heart of her childhood: and how she would gather around her other little children, and make *their* eyes bright and eager with many a wonderful tale, perhaps even with these very adventures of the little Alice of long-ago: and how she would feel with all their simple sorrows, and find a pleasure in all their simple joys, remembering her own child-life, and the happy summer days.

Opposite, the genesis of *Alice*: Folly Bridge (*top*) was the starting-point for a summer excursion up-river to Godstow (*bottom*), during which Carroll improvised almost the whole of the *Wonderland* story to amuse his three young passengers, Alice, Lorina and Edith Liddell. His colleague Duckworth (*top left*) was the other oarsman. *Right*, the last page of Carroll's original manuscript carries as an endpiece his portrait of the little girl who, by insisting that he should 'write out Alice's adventures for me', ensured the story's immortality.

So the chief characters participated in the mythology of that summer day, the Golden Afternoon created by the poet as the vehicle for his tale. Whatever the Met Office had to say about it, the weather must have been at least promising enough after luncheon for Carroll, who had been entertaining acquaintances, to change and gather together his picnic party.

Duckworth testified to the tale's spontaneity: 'I rowed *stroke* and he rowed *bow* . . . and the story was actually composed and spoken *over my shoulder* for the benefit of Alice Liddell, who was acting as "cox" of our gig.' Carroll afterwards told him 'that he sat up nearly the whole night, committing to a ms book his recollections of the drolleries. . . .'

Drolleries indeed! The tale went round the world, translated into some fifty languages, and proliferates to this day in all the media and on the lips of most English-speaking politicians. Carroll drew the first illustrations himself, accepted that they were not quite good enough, and became a tyrant to his professional illustrators. He insisted on visual aids for all his poetical and fictional work. He was all for the adaptation of *Alice* to the stage. He was no reactionary when it came to typewriters, fountain pens and phonographs. Probably he would have welcomed the recording, broadcasting and filming of his work in this century, though he might well have baulked at the thirteen writers employed by Walt Disney to rewrite *Alice*.

Alice, of course, lives on despite the interpretations by media and pundits. Six years before she materialized in words, Carroll jotted down a thought which provides a clue but not an explanation of the inspired mystery of the Alice world:

Query: when we are dreaming and, as so often happens, have a dim consciousness of the fact and try to wake, do we not say and do things which in waking life would be insane? May we not then sometimes define insanity as an inability to distinguish which is the waking and which the sleeping life? We often dream without the least suspicion of unreality: 'Sleep hath its own world', and it is often as lifelike as the other.

AS ONE WHO was a boy for much of his adult life he was by our standards something of a fuddy-duddy in his youth. He was seventeen when he wrote: 'I have got a new hat which I suppose Papa will not object to, as my old one was getting very shabby. . . . I have also got a pair of gloves, as I found I had not one pair of summer gloves, as I thought I had.'

Opposite, Carroll's own version of Alice about to enter the door in the tree (a subject not used by Tenniel).

This was written in May 1849 from the far-from-cosy surroundings of Rugby School. Another pupil ten years his senior, Thomas

Hughes, had recently passed through that establishment, and was to publish anonymously *Tom Brown's School Days* eight years before Dodgson, as Lewis Carroll, published *Alice in Wonderland*. The two Old Rugbeians did not meet until 1876, when they were introduced briefly at the office of Macmillan, the publisher, where Carroll was autographing eighty presentation copies of *The Hunting of the Snark*. Carroll's journal does not record any talk about the old school then, though he shared Hughes's critical attitude towards it. Almost his only comment was: 'I cannot say that I look back upon my life at a Public School with any sensations of pleasure or that any earthly considerations would induce me to go through my three years again.' He was slightly more explicit when referring to a cubicle system he had seen in after years in another school: '... if I had been thus secure from annoyance at night the hardships of the daily life would have been comparative trifles to bear.'

Whatever the hardships of the classrooms by day and of the dormitory by night (amazing that no treatise on sexual deviation has been devoted to that 'annoyance' at night) summer gloves were worn on a May morning and were a matter to be worried about in a school-boy letter home. Mrs Dodgson's 'dearest Charlie', the schoolboy

Below and *opposite*, Rugby School offered a bleak, brutal environment for the sheltered boy, whose anxiety over losing his gloves was later to characterize *Wonderland*'s White Rabbit (Carroll's illustration).

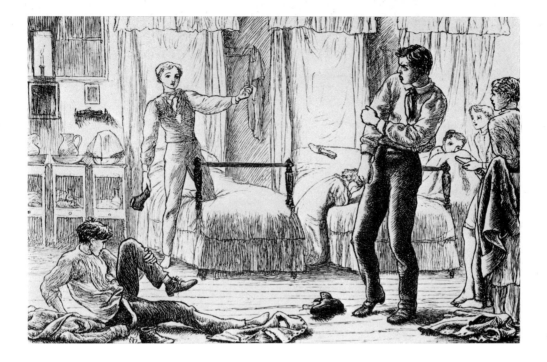

who became Lewis Carroll, was fussily, harmlessly, obsessed with the necessity of wearing gloves summer and winter when going out-doors. They were one of the small fastidious props of his world, a world of indoors, of college quarters, comfortable homes, art galleries, theatres, railway carriages. Outdoors was a health-orientated walk, an emotionally stimulating river excursion or seaside stroll, a Carroll-devised game of croquet, a carefully organized, luggage-accompanied journey in the south of England, with a few trips to the north and, surprisingly, one visit to Russia – the only venture abroad. Except for the straw boater for the river outings, a top hat was always worn and gloves carried. The loss of the first would be unthinkable: the mislaying or lack of the latter would cause the sort of anxiety echoed in the anguish of the White Rabbit, 'where can I have dropped them, I wonder?'

He was brought up in a world where there were not only sisters but servants to find things – and servants were to persist. His father, taking over Croft Rectory, his second boyhood home, had written that 'it puts an end to all hope of reducing my Establishment – it will be necessary to increase it by one Female, a sort of half Housemaid half Kitchenmaid.' So it was natural enough for the White Rabbit to cry: 'Mary Ann! Mary Ann! Fetch me my gloves this moment.' And for Alice to say to herself: 'He took me for his housemaid. . . . How sur-prised he'll be when he finds out who I am!'

17, 18. Seventeen, Eighteen, Maids in waiting.

Maids in abundance: the comfortable, hierarchical background which Lewis Carroll inherited, and accepted without question, necessarily included a large domestic staff.

If it should seem odd at first that a seventeen-year-old schoolboy should be writing rather poignantly about gloves, it soon becomes apparent there was nothing that did not go into his letters as he matured to become one of the most meticulous and persistent of letter-writers recorded in the English language. Perhaps indeed the record-holder. When he was twenty-nine years old he began a letter register keeping count of, and even summarizing, every incoming and outgoing letter. 'I *have* to write about 2000 letters a year,' he admitted. In the course of thirty-seven years the register swelled to 98,721, the last number he recorded before he died in 1898. Eager to share as well as to seek knowledge at all levels, he composed a booklet entitled *Eight or Nine Wise Words About Letter-Writing*, which

'Fairy Cooks', a fancy dress picture taken in the 1870s, towards the end of his photographic career, records Carroll's version of the domestic theme.

included the advice to address and stamp the envelope *before* writing the letter. Methodical advice this, and surely no more methodical man ever sat down (though sometimes he stood) to put pen to paper. He was conscientious, meticulous, fastidious, pedantic. He drove his talents and his pen hard. *The Lewis Carroll Handbook* exhaustively lists 'all pieces and editions printed and issued by Dodgson from 1845 to 1898'. The tally comes to 255. From a celibate Oxford don with such qualities and such application, undistracted by war, revolution, international politics, economic stress, industry or even commerce, it is not surprising that many of these publications lacked divine afflatus. The list includes, for instance, *Lawn Tennis Tournaments: the True Method of Assigning Prizes, with a Proof of the Fallacy of*

The ●●●●

My 🦌 Ina,

Though 👁 don't give birthday presents, still 👁

April
... write a birthday ✉.

June
... came 2 your 🚪 2 wish U many happy returns of the day, 🛢 the 🐈 met me, ✋ took me for a 🐀, ✋ hunted me👉 and👉 till 🐾 could hardly 🏠 However somehow 👁 got into the 🏠, ✋ there a 🐁 met me, ✋ took me for a 🦊, and pelted me

16

the Present Method (1883); *An Elementary Treatise on Determinants* (1867); *The Principles of Parliamentary Representation* (1884), and *Circular Billiards for Two Players* (1889). Yet with a couple of tales intended for children, and some well-turned verse, Lewis Carroll created a dimension of fantasy and poetry which illuminated, exercised, and extended human imagination and thought.

It has often been pointed out that Lewis Carroll has been quoted, and misquoted, in public speeches almost as frequently as Shakespeare – who had nearly three centuries' start. Certainly Carroll must come second only to Shakespeare in the number and complexity of words that have been written about him. Unlike Shakespeare, who contented himself autobiographically with the uncomplicated, compassionate bisexuality of the sonnets, Carroll wrote a lot about himself. In the compulsive letter-writing, in the thirteen volumes of his diaries kept intermittently from 1854 till a few weeks before his death in 1898, in discursive prefaces, articles and other occasional literature, he exposed himself but revealed little of his most private life. Perhaps there was nothing to be revealed, no mystery within the clerical garb and the neat academic life style, no mystery even in his penchant for the company of pre-pubescent girls and situations which would now be trendily associated with a Lolita syndrome. The diaries are two-dimensional, a massively detailed monument of self-evasion.

Opposite, an inexhaustible letter-writer (perhaps the most prolific of all time) Carroll sent picture-word letters to his favourite children.

Within a few months of its publication *Through The Looking-Glass*'s Jabberwock was sufficiently famous to provide the theme of a *Punch* cartoon (March 1872).

"THE MONSTER SLAIN."

"AND HAST THOU SLAIN THE *WAGGA*-WOCK?
COME TO MY ARMS, MY BEAMISH BOY!"

[*Vide* "The Jabberwock," in *Through the Looking-Glass.*

17

So readers, critics, devotees, and specialists re-explore and re-interpret the heady structures he raised, and even the acres of building he left with no significant elevation. Surveying the mass of explanation and speculation, most of it focused upon *Alice* and the life of her creator, it would seem that humanity is bent upon revenge for having surrendered to the magic of the *Wonderland*, the *Looking Glass*, the *Snark*. What is this magic? Who was this man? What made him tick? Can a meaning be supplied for everything?

No wonder that *The Annotated Alice* and *The Annotated Snark*, both edited by Martin Gardner, should be best-selling paperbacks. Their entertaining scholarship is good fun, with no pretence that *Alice* and the *Snark* are just for children. In his own day Carroll became much bothered by demands for elucidation, and went on record with a good poet's answer. In 1880 he wrote, 'I have a letter from you ... asking me "Why don't you explain the *Snark*?" Let me answer it now – "because I can't". Are you able to explain things which you don't understand?'

Again, in 1896, twenty years after the poem was published, he wrote: 'As to the meaning of the *Snark*? I'm very much afraid I didn't mean anything but nonsense! Still, you know, words mean more than we mean to express when we use them: so a whole book

The opening mood of *Alice in Wonderland* is evoked in *The Woodman's Child* by Arthur Hughes, the Pre-Raphaelite artist and friend of Carroll.

18

ought to mean a great deal more than the writer meant. So, whatever good meanings are in the book, I'm very glad to accept as the meaning of the book.'

This, like so much of the man's character, was a shrewd over-simplification. He was a very private man who took good care of his public image. His acceptance of every convention in the environ-ment of a nineteenth-century Oxford don did not diminish public interest in him. With remarkable briskness, less than twelve months after his death, his nephew Stuart Dodgson Collingwood published the first of many biographical works, declaring: 'If this Memoir helps others of his admirers to a fuller knowledge of a man whom to know was to love, I shall not have written in vain.' Public interest

Carroll's portrait of Edith Liddell, Alice's younger sister, who died in 1876.

waned somewhat at the beginning of this century but picked up as an antidote to the horrors of the First World War, and has never abated since. Virginia Woolf offered a particularly discerning assessment of Carroll's perennial appeal:

If Oxford dons in the nineteenth century had an essence, he was that essence. He was so good that his sisters worshipped him; so pure that his nephew had nothing to say about him. . . . But this untinted jelly contained within it a perfectly hard crystal. It contained childhood. . . . It lodged in him whole and entire . . . he could do what no one else has ever been able to do – he could return to that world: he could re-create it, so that we too become children again . . . the two *Alices* are not books for children, they are the only books in which we become children. . . . '

This 'perfectly hard crystal' containing childhood was his true essential life, expressed in the *Alice* books and in some poems, and sustained always by successive child friends. When he spoke to these children he lost his habitual stammer. He simply became one of them, whether or not they accepted him – and most did. This perennial childhood, together with the fantasy and poetry that sometimes expressed it, was his reality. His forty-seven years of academic life at Christ Church, Oxford – thirty of them in the same rooms – were acceptable as a routine of living, a disciplined fantasy materially rewarding but emotionally unreal.

A poet's moments of creation, the sacred moments of fusion between complete concentration and total relaxation, between faculties and wonder – these are reality. Such was reality for Lewis Carroll. It was rare, not often repeated though much sought for. Its catalyst was little girls. Its product was profound fantasy, which has entertained and provoked adult minds, and bored and frightened many children with its childish guile.

This potent force, this reality of the poet Lewis Carroll, was fertilized in the serene clerical world into which Charles Lutwidge Dodgson was born on 27 January 1832. It was a time of political turbulence and social distress, with revolution in Europe, and Britain only saved from violence by the passage of that year's Reform Bill. Britain's first passenger-carrying railway was two years old, and in the first year or so of the boy's life the world changed rapidly. Slavery in the British Empire was abolished (with £20 million compensation for the owners in the colonies). The first effective Factory Act was passed, liberating British children under nine years of age from work in cotton mills. With the 1834 Poor Law, the State assumed responsibility for the workless, and when Victoria was crowned, and little Charles was just five, Charles Dickens began the serialization of his protest at the inhumanities of the system – *Oliver Twist*.

WHEN CHARLES was writing from school about his gloves he had just read the first instalment of 'Dickens' new tale', *David Copperfield* (1849): 'It purports to be his life and begins with his birth and child/hood: it seems a poor plot, but some of the characters and scenes are very good.'

The world of rural Cheshire, into which he was born at the parson/age out in the fields, a mile and a half from the village of Daresbury, was far removed from the social stresses endured and vehemently expressed by the young Dickens.

> *An island/farm – broad seas of corn*
> *Stirred by the wandering breath of morn –*
> *The happy spot where I was born.*

Such was Lewis Carroll's recollection of it, penned in a senti/mental poem, 'Faces in the Fire' (1860). He was the eldest boy of a family of four boys and seven girls born to the Revd Charles Dodgson

Iffley Mill, Oxford, was another favourite spot for river picnics. Apart from *Alice* itself, the stories Carroll told on these excursions 'lived and died, like summer midges, each in its own golden afternoon'.

The Dodgsons in silhouette:
Charles as a young boy, with (*right*) his
mother and father. *Below*, Daresbury
Parsonage in Cheshire, where he
spent his first years. Destroyed by a
fire, only a well-head now remains.

and Frances Jane Lutwidge, both socially well connected, cousins, belonging to families with strong traditions of service to the Anglican Church and to the Crown. They were aware of their position in the social order of nineteenth-century Britain, as was Alice when in danger of being mistaken for a housemaid in Wonderland. Awareness of class, ever-present but never snobbishly over-asserted, with the belief that better class people actually *looked* better, went along with Charles throughout his life. In his appalling epic *Sylvie and Bruno* he described two passengers on a railway station (in a passage he characteristically read aloud to the children of the Marquess of Salisbury in 1872): 'They were a young woman and a little girl: the former so far as one could judge by appearances, was a nursemaid, or possibly a nursery-governess, in attendance on the child, whose refined face, even more than her dress, distinguished her as of a higher class than her companion.'

At the Daresbury parsonage there was a proper sense of obligation. The Revd Charles Dodgson worked for the poor of the parish, ran a Sunday School, organized lectures, increased the size of his congregation, and started a mission among the barge folk working on a canal in the parish. With the financial assistance of a local landowner, Lord Francis Egerton, he converted one of the barges to a chapel.

During the sixteen years at Daresbury there was not much money to spare for the parson and his family of eleven (one more child arrived later). He supplemented his income by taking pupils.

The Revd Charles Dodgson was not cut out to be a rustic clerical nonentity. His portrait shows an ample, handsome, authoritarian figure. He was a classical scholar, took a Double First at Christ Church, published a number of religious books and, according to Collingwood, 'mathematics were his favourite pursuit'. After being appointed chaplain to the bishop of Ripon he was elevated in due course to become archdeacon of Richmond and a canon of Ripon Cathedral. He was indeed a potent father figure. Collingwood, who had known him personally, described him as 'a man of deep piety and of a somewhat reserved and grave disposition which however was tempered by the most generous charity. . . . In moments of relaxation his wit and humour were the delight of his clerical friends, for he had the rare power of telling anecdotes effectively.'

Charles inherited certain of his father's noble features and all of his piety – manifested for instance in this letter to a friend, written in 1897:

The favour I would ask is, that you will not tell me any more stories, such as you did on Friday, of remarks which children are said to have made on very sacred subjects – remarks which most people would recognise as irreverent, if made by *grown-up people* . . . I simply ask it as a personal favour to myself. The hearing of that anecdote gave me so much pain, and spoiled so much the pleasure of my tiny dinner-party, that I feel sure you will kindly spare me such in future.

At about the same time, during the last months of his life, Charles wrote consoling another friend: 'The greatest blow that has ever fallen on *my* life was the death, nearly thirty years ago, of my own dear father.' His lifelong and sometimes self-indulgent concern with reverence no doubt stemmed from the father figure. But his father also contributed a splendidly exaggerated sense of fun, with a truly Carrollian measure of off-with-his-head ruthlessness. Here are extracts from a letter sent from the father to his son Charlie, aged eight:

I will not forget your commission. As soon as I get to Leeds I shall scream out in the middle of the street, *Ironmongers – Iron-mongers* – Six hundred men will rush out of their shops in a moment – fly, fly, in all directions – ring the bells, call the constables – set the town on fire. I *will* have a file & a screw-driver, & a ring, & if they are not brought directly, in forty seconds I will leave nothing but one small cat alive in the whole town of Leeds, & I shall only leave that, because I am afraid I shall not have time to kill it.

Then what a bawling & a tearing of hair there will be! Pigs & babies, camels & butterflies, rolling in the gutter together – old women rushing up the chimneys & cows after them – ducks hiding themselves in coffee cups, &

Archdeacon Dodgson, who bequeathed to his son a surrealistic sense of humour in addition to the more orthodox virtues of piety and industry.

fat geese trying to squeeze themselves into pencil cases – at last the Mayor of Leeds will be found in a soup plate covered up with custard & stuck full of almonds to make him look like a sponge cake that he may escape the dreadful destruction of the Town. . . .

The letter ends with this flourish: 'At last they bring the things which I ordered & then I spare the Town & send off in fifty waggons & under the protection of 10,000 soldiers, a file & a screw-driver and a ring as a present to Charles Lutwidge Dodgson from his affec^{nte} Papa.'

Mama, Frances Jane Lutwidge, 'one of the sweetest and gentlest women that ever lived' according to one contemporary, undoubtedly bequeathed the gentleness which balanced the sterner qualities of Papa. She was duly celebrated by her eldest and favourite son in his 'Easter Greeting', in which he recalled 'a Mother's gentle hand that undraws your curtains and a Mother's sweet voice that summons you to rise'.

Mama's letters gushed with haste and affection. Charles treasured what was probably the first he received from her, addressed from Hull,

'My Dearest Charlie' but meant for them all: 'All your notes have delighted me, my precious children. . . . I am happy to say your dearest Papa is quite well – his cough is rather *tickling*, but it is of no consequence. It delights me, my darling Charlie, to hear that you are getting on so well with your Latin, and that you make so few mistakes in your Exercises. Give . . . all my treasures, including yourself, 1,000,000,000 kisses from me; with my most affectionate love. . . . '

A lifetime later, in 1890, he was writing to his 'pet' Isa Bowman in violet ink ('dreadfully ugly', she thought) after she and her sister had sent him 'millions of kisses' in a letter:

My own Darling, It's all very well for you and Nellie and Emsie to write in millions of hugs and kisses, but please consider the *time* it would occupy your poor old very busy Uncle! Try hugging and kissing Emsie for a minute by the watch, and I don't think you'll manage it more than 20 times a minute. 'Millions' must mean 2 millions at least.

20)2,000,000 hugs and kisses
60)100,000 minutes
12(1,666 hours
6)138 days (at twelve hours a day)
23 weeks.

I couldn't go on hugging and kissing more than 12 hours a day: and I wouldn't like to spend *Sundays* that way. So you see it would take 23 *weeks* of hard work. Really, my dear child, I *cannot spare the time.*

It was Mama who brought into his life the whimsy which never left him. The phonetic baby-talk that sometimes went with it derived from his earliest nursery days, and appears with somebody guiding his hand in the first of his surviving letters, addressed to his nurse:

'My dear Bun, I love you very much & tend you a kitt from little Charlie with the horn of hair. I'd like to give you a kitt, but I tan't, betause I'm at Marke. What a long letter I've written. I'm twite tired.'

And so the awful phonetically lisping child Bruno, a lifetime later, was made to say, 'I slipted down the bank. And I tripted over a stone. And the stone hurted my foot. . . . Why does there be stones? Mister Sir, does oo know?' *Alice*, coming in the years between, mercifully escaped the excruciating oo business which wove its way through both the *Sylvie and Bruno* books. But then *Alice* was the pure magic distillation of all childhood which Carroll carried with him from the Daresbury parsonage, to Croft Rectory, and into the world.

'Even the passing of a cart was a matter of great interest to the children', wrote Collingwood of the home where Charlie spent those deeply significant first eleven years of his life. 'He made pets of the most odd and unlikely animals and numbered certain snails and toads among his intimate friends.' He was in fact accumulating the realities of Wonderland. The Dodgson family was a self-sufficient unit, with affectionate outer circles of relatives elsewhere. All Saints Church, Daresbury, to which they walked across the flat fields on Sunday to listen to Papa taking the service, has been restored since their day – with a Lewis Carroll window added – but retains its character much as they knew it. The Jacobean oak pulpit from which Papa held forth is rich with carved angels and grotesques. One of these, which surely impressed its image on Charlie's mind, is a gryphon – to be rediscovered in Wonderland lying in the sun and occasionally exclaiming 'Hjckrrh!'. The parsonage itself 'mid seas of corn' was burnt down in the 1880s, its site being marked by a small plaque in the lane, and the remains of a well-head in a field. It is still a solitary place, though only a few miles away there is the Lord Daresbury Hotel with a Lewis Carroll Banqueting Suite, a Looking Glass Restaurant, and a ceramic mural eight feet high depicting characters from *Wonderland*.

In 1843 the Dodgsons left that Cheshire countryside which had scarcely noticed the industrial revolution in Warrington seven miles away. A living at Croft on the Yorkshire-Durham borders fell vacant. It was in the gift of the Crown, which meant that the prime minister, Sir Robert Peel, had the disposal of it, on the advice of the bishop of Ripon. The landowning classes had a say in such Church matters, and Lord Francis Egerton weighed in with a letter to Peel:

Mr Dodgson has held for 16 years a small living in Cheshire in which I have some property. I am able from this circumstance to bear testimony to the zeal & efficiency with which he has discharged his office since I became acquainted with the district in question, & the care which he has extended to a very generally neglected but not ungrateful class, that of the canal navigators.

For the prime minister, the next best thing to being a man of God was evidently to appoint men of God. He wrote a personal letter, resounding with high principles, to Dodgson declaring: 'I have resolved to appoint you to the Living of Croft. . . . I make the offer to you upon the full understanding, in the case of a Living of so much value, that you will be enabled to reside upon the Living and to discharge the Parochial Duties in Person.'

So, unwittingly, Peel laid down for Charles the solid foundations of his world of security, acceptance, duty, convention, domesticity, family loyalty, and Anglican clerical probity – and a second magic period of juvenescence. His father's living was worth some £900 a year – enough for a generous family life with no lack of domestic servants. The Rectory was spacious. In this century, a little altered but unspoiled, it is divided to make two homes. For the Dodgson family

The Gryphon, as it appears in Carroll's manuscript version of *Alice*, may have been inspired by carvings on the oak pulpit at Daresbury.

Croft Rectory, with croquet on the lawn for the Dodgson family and friends. Today the Rectory remains outwardly very little changed.

of two adults and ten children there were ample bedrooms, four reception rooms, nursery, kitchen with such agreeable elaborations as butler's pantry, housekeeper's room, needlework room, men-servants' room, servants' hall, and bacon house. Close to the house was – and is – an ancient yew known as the 'umbrella tree', which in due course furnished the title of Charles's famous 'very local' magazine, *The Rectory Umbrella*.

The Rectory epitomized mid-Victorian professional class virtue and well-being. The family was self-entertaining and tribal. Only towards his mother and father did Charles show really deep attachment. Family relationships, however, were strong, widespread and lasting. Charles was to become meticulous in maintaining his responsibilities as head of the tribe.

In his boyhood years at Croft, from 1843 till his establishment for the rest of his life in Oxford in 1851, Charles led the tribe in childish pursuits, storing up within his psyche the essential magic and poetry of youth. 'The children of the North,' he called this tribe, celebrating them in *The Rectory Umbrella*:

Above, 'the children of the North':
six of the seven Dodgson sisters, with
his youngest brother Edwin in the
centre. A study taken by Carroll in
1857.

The Rectory Umbrella frontispiece.
Manuscript magazines irregularly
produced by Carroll during the
Croft years foreshadowed much of
his later fantasy:

> All day he sat without a hat,
> That comical old feller,
> Shading his form from the driving
>   storm
> With the Rectory Umbrella.

Fair stands the ancient Rectory,
The Rectory of Croft,
The sun shines bright upon it,
The breezes whisper soft.

From all the house and garden,
Its inhabitants come forth,
And muster in the road without,
And pace in twos and threes about,
The children of the North. . . .

There was the sibling ruthlessness expected in the nursery of large families, just as the cook with a mind of her own was taken for granted in the kitchens. Aspects of the youthful poem 'Brother and Sister', written at Croft when Charles was thirteen and now largely forgotten, were to re-emerge potently in *Wonderland*:

'Sister, sister, go to bed!
Go and rest your weary head.'
Thus the prudent brother said.

'Do you want a battered hide,
Or scratches to your face applied?'
Thus his sister calm replied. . . .

Off to the cook he quickly ran.
'Dear Cook, please lend a frying-pan
To me as quickly as you can.'

'And wherefore should I lend it you?'
'The reason, Cook, is plain to view.
I wish to make an Irish stew.'

'What meat is in that stew to go?'
'My sister'll be the contents!'
                    'Oh!'
'You'll lend the pan to me, Cook?'
                    'No!'

One of Carroll's earliest illustrations from *The Rectory Umbrella*.

The year before they all arrived at Croft, Queen Victoria had written from Buckingham Palace to the King of the Belgians: 'We arrived here yesterday morning, having come by the railroad, from Windsor, in half an hour, free from dust and crowd and heat, and I am quite charmed with it.' Though the Duke of Wellington had deplored the notion of railways on a national scale because 'they would encourage the lower classes to move about', the public, undeterred by the revolutionary threat, followed the speculators in the railway mania, a bubble which reached its peak and burst in 1846, leaving many ruined but the countryside networked by the new

wonder of steam. And three decades later Lewis Carroll made its echo ring mockingly six times – and for all time – through *The Hunting of the Snark*:

Bridging the Tees near Croft, Britain's first commercial railway ran within a few miles of the Rectory. From the beginning Carroll was at home in the steam age.

> They sought it with thimbles, they sought it with care;
>   They pursued it with forks and hope;
> They threatened its life with a railway-share;
> They charmed it with smiles and soap.

The children of the North were a bare four miles from the birth-place of it all, the Stockton–Darlington railway. The main line passed within earshot. They were indeed the children of the railway age, the first generation to take for granted the existence of the new, still exciting, iron roads. Charles was to live with a Bradshaw Rail-way Guide always at his elbow.

In the Rectory grounds he devised a railway game for his brothers and sisters. The train was made up with a wheelbarrow, a barrel and a small truck. Stations were placed at intervals in the walled kitchen gardens, with rules penned by Charles: 'Station master must mind his station, and supply refreshments: he can put anyone who behaves badly to prison, while a train goes round the garden: he must ring for the passengers to take their seats, then count 20 slowly, then ring again for the train to start. . . . '

Thus railway lore was consolidated in the life of the boy Charles, to become constantly and pedantically used by the Revd C. L. Dodgson. It participated in the magic of Lewis Carroll's poetic fantasy when Alice, in *Through The Looking-Glass*, suddenly finds

The railway entered the Victorian imagination at many levels: in the comfortable domesticity of the reserved compartment, in the grandiose architecture of the station hotel, or (*opposite*) in children's educational books.

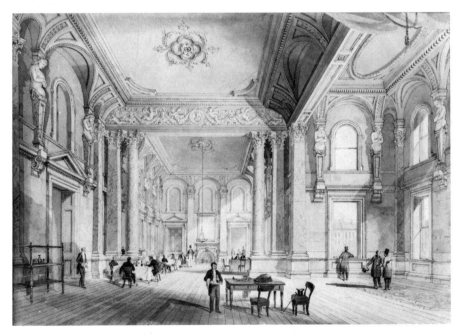

herself in the railway carriage without a ticket: 'A Goat that was sitting next to the gentleman in white, shut his eyes and said in a loud voice, "she ought to know her way to the ticket-office, even if she doesn't know her alphabet!"'

It also provided at least one theme for another diversion, the marionette theatre which the boy constructed with the aid of the village carpenter. *La Guida di Bragia*, a ballad opera based upon Bradshaw, was one of the most popular of the works written by Charles for his puppet troupe. Papa disapproved of life-size theatre. In his view *no* clergyman should ever set foot in one, no matter whether it were serious or frivolous. Home theatricals and marionette performances escaped this censure, so Charles the impresario delighted his adoring audiences and established his own lifelong adoration for the theatre, that is for the acting and the staging more than the play itself.

His own passion for words was precociously manifest in the domestic journalism devised for the children of the North. These family manuscript magazines were almost entirely written, edited and illustrated by Charles. His drawings were zestful, witty, accomplished, yet, as he fortunately realized before too long, not quite up to the professional standards of the time. Those done at Croft are if anything more lively and appealing than those made for the first draft of *Wonderland*, and the sadly conventional later ones. He remained talented enough to bully, inspire, supervise, encourage and exasperate artists he was fortunate in finding as collaborators.

The first of the Croft magazines, *Useful and Instructive Poetry*, appeared when Charles was thirteen. There was a typical touch of

A nineteenth-century English marionette familiar to Carroll.

tribal ruthlessness in the poem called 'Rules and Regulations'. First the couplet:

> *Learn well your grammar*
> *And never stammer . . .*

And later:

> *Eat bread with butter.*
> *Once more, don't stutter.*

Charles himself was afflicted with a stammer which, except in the presence of his child friends, never left him or responded to treatment. Several of his brothers and sisters also suffered.

Other magazines were *The Comet, The Rosebud, The Star, The Will-o'-the-Wisp*: and these children of the North also left non-literary mementoes of their tribal life. When Croft Rectory was being altered in 1950 a remarkable cache was discovered beneath the floor-boards of the second-floor room which had been their nursery. The items brought out of hiding after more than a hundred years included a pen-knife, a hair-slide, various bits of china and, more significantly, a child's left shoe, a thimble, and a child's white glove in perfect condition after its long rest. There was one of those messages which nineteenth-century workmen delighted to leave hidden for another generation: 'This floor was laid by Mr Martin and Mr Sutton June 19th, 1843.' With it, pencilled in Charles's handwriting was his note to posterity:

> *And we'll wander through*
> *the wide world*
> *and chase the buffalo.*

This of course is exactly what he did. While his quirky, celibate, donnish, puzzle-loving, child-doting, conformist personality accepted the unreality of forty-seven years in the dismal, past-haunted conventional world of Christ Church, his reality was the wide world and the magic chase of the buffalo.

Long before the cache was discovered, some of the items had emerged as part of the stuff of his poetry. The White Rabbit of course possessed 'two or three pairs of tiny white kid-gloves'. The Dodo presented Alice with her own thimble, amid applause, saying: 'We beg your acceptance of this elegant thimble.' (Succinctly described by Derek Hudson as 'the *locus classicus* of thimble literature'.) The White Knight's song included a 'left-hand shoe' and a buffalo:

> *And now, if e'er by chance I put*
> *My fingers into glue,*
> *Or madly squeeze a right-hand foot*
> *Into a left-hand shoe . . .*

And later on the 'old man' is said to have 'snorted like a buffalo'.

An 'elegant thimble' (one of the objects recently found in a cache beneath the Croft nursery floorboards) was presented to Alice by the Dodo (a reference to Carroll when he stammered – Do-Do-Dodgson).

Croft Rectory still contains another intriguing Carrollian clue, left by other workmen and recently rediscovered. There is a skylight type of window on the top floor (now a self-contained flat), which Charles would have been able to look up and see across the passage from his bedroom door. Scrawled on the window pane are these artisan signatures:

> *John Stobbart Bongate Darlington*
> *T Young Painted July 23 1836*
> *Plumer an Glazer an Tiner 24 August 1830*
> *Edward Johnson Plumber Darlington 1834*

These good men were outside the house when they wrote. Seen from within their message is mirror-written. Could they thus have sown the seeds of *Through The Looking-Glass*?

There is also just one place name which may have made a particular impression upon the boy Charles. Some thirty miles from Croft is Beamish, with a very grand mine-owner's mansion which was flourishing in his time, and in this is an open air museum, surely immortalized, however, in the poem begun in mirror-writing, 'Jabberwocky' – 'Come to my arms, my beamish boy!'

At the end of his first year at Croft, Charles started to go away to school. He took to education, though not to schooling. He did not rebel or even complain over much. He suffered, like thousands of privileged youths then and since, the rigours of the public school system. His appetite for knowledge was rapacious. Collingwood noted early evidence of this: ' . . . when Charles was a very small boy, he came up to his father and showed him a book of logarithms, with the request, "Please explain". Mr Dodgson told him that he was much too young to understand anything about such a difficult subject. The child listened to what his father said, and appeared to think it irrelevant, for he still insisted, "But, please, explain!"'

Three months before his death Charles wrote in his journal: '*Die notandus* [*sic*]. Discovered a rule for dividing a number by 9, by mere addition and subtraction. I felt sure there must be an analogous one for 11, and found it, and proved the first rule by Algebra, after working about nine hours!'

His first boarding-school was nine miles from home at Richmond, Yorkshire. He arrived at the age of twelve, two years before the town was connected to the railway in 1846. It was an old-fashioned school, as Collingwood was at some pains to point out, but fortunately tough enough to provide an initiation for Rugby. Collingwood tells us: 'Long after he left school his name was remembered as that of a boy who knew well how to use his fists in defence of a righteous cause.' Charles's first impressions are preserved in a letter he wrote to his two eldest sisters:

I hope you are all getting on well, as also the sweet twins, the boys I think that I like the best, are Harry Austin, and all the Tates of which there are 7 besides a little girl who came down to dinner the first day, but not since, and I also like Edmund Tremlet, and William and Edward Swire, Tremlet is a sharp little fellow about 7 years old, the youngest in the school, I also like Kemp and Mawley. . . . I have had 3 misfortunes in my clothes etc. 1st I cannot find my tooth-brush, so that I have not brushed my teeth for 3 or 4 days, 2nd I cannot find my blotting paper, and 3rd I have no shoe-horn. The chief games are, football, wrestling, leap frog, and fighting. Excuse bad writing.

Yr affec' brother Charles.

Charles stayed for a year and a half, and afterwards referred to Tate as his 'kind old schoolmaster'. Tate's valedictory note said: 'Be assured that I shall always feel a peculiar interest in the gentle, intelligent, and well-conducted boy who is now leaving us.'

There followed a schooling befitting the son of a well-found, well-connected and well-educated cleric – at Rugby where the famous Dr Thomas Arnold had proclaimed: 'What we must look for here is, 1st, religious and moral principles: 2ndly, gentlemanly conduct: 3rdly, intellectual ability.' Here Charles won many prizes for work, was no good at games, and came through unscathed. Some six years later he wrote: 'During my stay I made I suppose some progress in learning of various kinds, but none of it was done *con amore*, and I spent an incalculable time in writing out impositions – this last I consider one of the chief faults of Rugby School. I made some friends there.'

On his departure there was another glowing report to Papa – from Dr Tait, who had succeeded Arnold as headmaster and was to become Archbishop of Canterbury. 'I must not allow your son to leave school without expressing to you the very high opinion I entertain of him. . . . His mathematical knowledge is great for his age . . . his examination for the Divinity prize was one of the most creditable exhibitions I have ever seen.'

For a year Charles was back at Croft preparing for Oxford, and producing *The Rectory Umbrella*. There is little record of this ending of his boyhood, this last year as a child of the North before his translation for the rest of his life to Oxford and, in due course, the emergence of Lewis Carroll. It could well have been a very important period of integration with childhood and family life. He had endured Rugby and now he shook it off. It was as if the whole of his schooling had been clothing, to be discarded with relief – but having served a useful purpose. His love of learning, his appetite for knowledge, had been immensely enhanced by this schooling, backed always by the home teaching and advice of Papa. Now it was gratefully forgotten and rarely afterwards recollected. The society of sisters, of younger brothers, of the gentle mother, of the learned, benign, deeply respected Papa, the serenity and security of it all, this was the essence that Charles carried with him into his adult life – from a lesser to a greater sheltered world. After only three years he was writing, in 'Solitude', somewhat maudlin valedictory lines:

> I'd give all wealth that years have piled,
> The slow result of Life's decay,
> To be once more a little child
> For one bright summer-day.

He was well equipped and endowed. He was presentable, nearly six feet tall, with a trim figure (too thin in later life), with good features, a handsome full face inherited from Papa. He was always neatly dressed, top-hatted and, as we have noted, garnished with winter and summer gloves. He never wore an overcoat. He was shyly gregarious – among his social equals. His stammer did not affect his social life though it hampered his public utterances, especially preaching. Infantile fever had left him deaf in one ear. He always sat on the extreme right of any auditorium, and one of his child friends recalled that he always liked her to walk on his left.

Learned works, even books, have been written about his physical and mental health. Dr Selwyn H. Goodacre, in an authoritative work entitled *The Illnesses of Lewis Carroll*, stated: 'By concentrating

West Front of

on Lewis Carroll's illnesses throughout his life, one may get the impression that he was unhealthy. This is quite erroneous. Generally speaking, he was fit apart from the years 1885 to 1891, when he suffered a number of ailments largely brought on by the particular tensions of life at that time. . . . Speaking as a general practitioner, I feel that Charles Dodgson would have been an excellent patient: troubling his doctor only when absolutely necessary, and always accepting the advice given. . . . '

So Oxford accepted a young man who was healthy enough, a keen mathematician, studious, hard-working and, by inclination and up-bringing, conformist. A measure of eccentricity, so long as it was moral, was acceptable too. To his father Dr Jelf, one of the canons of Christ Church, purred: 'I am sure I express the common feeling of all who remember you at Christ Church when I say that we shall rejoice to see a son of yours worthy to tread in your footsteps.'

CHARLES WAS NINETEEN when he arrived at 'the House', and sixty-six when he left it to die in Guildford. Only one trip abroad, routine vacations, family matters, affairs and entertainment in London took him away – always briefly – from Oxford, from his college, from his devotion to mathematics.

John Ruskin, who had preceded him there by a few years and was to become a somewhat tentative friend and adviser on illustrations for the *Snark*, wrote:

On the whole, of important places and services for the Christian souls of England, the choir of Christ Church was at that epoch of English history virtually the navel and seat of life. . . . In this choir, written so closely and consecutively with indisputable British history, met every morning a con-gregation representing the best of what Britain had become – orderly as the crew of a man-of-war, in the goodly ship of their temple. Every man in his place, according to his age, rank, and learning; every man of sense or heart there recognizing that he was either fulfilling, or being prepared to fulfill, the gravest duties required of Englishmen.

Ruskin did not lower his vision to aspects of medievalism, which lingered on in the person of a verger who ran a beer store in a cup-board beneath a pew, and who was to be seen at the entrance of the cathedral choir, armed with a whip to see off the dogs following their young masters to prayers.

Within a month or so of his arrival Charles wrote home a spirited account of these university dogs, providing a foretaste of Carrollian narrative skill:

This afternoon I was sitting in my room when I heard a sudden shrieking of dogs, as if fighting: I rushed to the window, but the fight, if any, was over,

Opposite, Christ Church College, Oxford, as it appeared at the time of Carroll's arrival in 1851.

having lasted for about the space of 3 seconds, and every thing & every body was flying from the scene of combat: six dogs went headlong down the steps, which lead into the quad, yelling at the very top of their voices: six sticks came flying after them, & after that came their six masters, all running their hardest, and all in different directions. For a little time none of the dogs knew which way to go, so they went darting about, tumbling over each other, screaming, & getting hit by the sticks, & their masters did the same only they screamed in a different manner: at last 3 dogs got away & ran straight home, screaming as they went, 2 others were hunted up & down the quad by their masters, I suppose with the intention of beating them, but were never sufficiently caught for that purpose, & the sixth went home with its master, but even *it* screamed all the way. Never was such desperate vengeance taken for so small an offence. . . .

Incidentally, Collingwood tells us Charles 'never seemed to care about animals. . . . He hated, indeed, to see them ill-treated in any way, and would go out of his way to relieve their distress when he could. . . . But he never kept pets of any sort.'

The start of his undergraduate career was blighted by the sudden death of his mother. The size of her family, and of the Rectory responsibilities, wore her out. Yet there was no unhappiness in her: ' . . . she spoke most touchingly and beautifully of the responsibility incurred by the lot of so much happiness,' wrote a close relative, 'and that it really at times was "alarming" to look round her and feel that she had not a wish unfulfilled.'

Outwardly, Charles bore this loss with restraint. Back at Oxford he wrote with a light touch to the stricken household at Croft – the story of the dog fight. Inwardly, his sense of loss continued deep, from time to time emerging in his verse. Two years later, for instance, he was writing:

Here may the silent tears I weep
Lull the vexed spirit into rest,
As infants sob themselves to sleep
Upon a mother's breast.

Anyone who has lost a parent while at school or college learns to wrap away the pain lest the embarrassed compassion of one's fellows adds to the weight of bereavement. Charles undemonstratively made many acquaintances and few close friends, watched but did not play games, and worked conscientiously towards an academic career, bearing in mind that his father was comfortably off but not wealthy, and had three other sons to educate. In 1851 he won a Boulter scholarship, and the following year obtained a First Class Honours in mathematics and a Second in classical moderations. He wrote home to his sister Elizabeth, 'I am getting quite tired of being congratulated on various subjects: there seems no end to it. If I had shot the Dean, I could hardly have had more said about it.'

Far from outraging authority, he acquired a Studentship, the equivalent of a Fellowship at Christ Church, nominated by the formidable controversialist and High Churchman, Dr Edward Bouverie Pusey (1800–82), Regius Professor of Hebrew and canon of Christ Church. He was an old friend of Archdeacon Dodgson, to whom he wrote: 'I have great pleasure in telling you that I have been enabled to recommend your son. . . . One of the Censors brought me to-day five names; but in their minds it was plain that they thought your son on the whole the most eligible for the College.'

All unsuspecting the brilliance of the flash his son was capable of emitting, Mr Dodgson wrote to Charles: ' . . . it is the steady, pains-taking, likely-to-do-good man, who in the long run wins the race against those who now and then give a brilliant flash and, as Shake-speare says, "straight are cold again" . . . your affectionate heart will derive no small amount of joy from thinking of the joy which you have occasioned to me, and to all the circle of your home.'

No explicit mention in these letters that Christ Church Students were required to take holy orders and not to marry. Mr Dodgson was clearly more flattered by his son's success than worried by succession. There can be little doubt about Dr Pusey's satisfaction. A contem-porary wrote that Pusey 'made an idol of celibacy. His obscurantist dread of worldly influence begot the feeling that no young woman was safe except in a nunnery, no man except in orders.' Significantly he added: ' . . . if only the youth were pious, earnest, docile, the great thing was to fix, to secure, to *capture* him.'

Thus was little Charlie translated into manhood, willingly captured in a world in which Anglicanism loomed, with clerical giants often in the throes of battle with one another. Oxford was the battleground. His sponsor Pusey, as leader of the Oxford Movement, had been suspended from the office of university preacher for three years in 1843. Pusey's friend and former ally, John Henry Newman, had resigned his Oxford living to join the Roman Catholic Church in 1845 – to become in after years a cardinal and the writer of an appreciative letter about *The Hunting of the Snark*. Henry Edward Manning, former Oxford preacher, resigned his archdeaconry to become a Roman Catholic – and ultimately a cardinal – in the year Charles arrived in Oxford. Closer than most to Charles was Samuel Wilberforce, bishop of Oxford, regarded as a holy terror by some for his reactionary views and by some called 'Soapy Sam'. He was photo-graphed – looking tense – by Lewis Carroll, and from Jowett drew the comment: 'Samuel of Oxford is not unpleasing if you will resign yourself to be semi-humbugged by a semi-humbug.' But the most immediate and constant ecclesiastical presence in the life and work of Charles Dodgson was Henry George Liddell, dean of Christ Church 1855–91.

While the battles within the established Church thundered round the head of this parsonage-bred young man, he managed to maintain a middle moderate course of Anglicanism. It was comfortable, rigorous though undemanding, knew a gentleman when it saw one, and was beginning to detach itself from the industrial masses. It consolidated in the lifetime of Charles as a sedate structure of national respectability and conformism – and he was to serve it faithfully, looking neither to right nor to left.

Only a few letters survive to tell us a little of his life as an undergraduate before his meticulous diary-writing began. His first impression of the 1851 Great Exhibition in the Crystal Palace in Hyde Park was 'one of bewilderment. It looks like a sort of fairyland. . . . ' His love of gadgetry and popular science was most stimulated by his uncle, Skeffington Lutwidge. A barrister and a Commissioner in Lunacy by profession, this much-loved bachelor was described in action in a letter from Charles to his sister in June 1852:

He has as usual got a number of new oddities, including a lathe, telescope stand, crest stamp (see the top of this note-sheet), a beautiful little pocket instrument for measuring distances on a map, refrigerator, &c., &c. We had an observation of the moon and Jupiter last night, & afterwards live animalculae in his large microscope: this is a most interesting sight, as the creatures are most conveniently transparent, & you see all kinds of organs jumping about like a complicated piece of machinery, & even the circulation of the blood. Everything goes on at railway speed, so I suppose they must be some of those insects that only live a day or two, & try to make the most of it.

Uncle Skeffington was to play an important part in involving Charles in photography, one of his life's obsessions. Much of Charles's pleasure in innovation, improvement of systems, and the more trivial machinery of living, can probably be traced to the influence of Uncle Skeffington. His early acceptance of the typewriter for part at least of his voluminous correspondence was evidence of his continuing appetite for the technical advances of his century – so long as they were applicable to his way of life. When in 1890 he went, two days running, to an exhibition of Edison's phonograph, he wrote in his diary: 'It is a pity that we are not fifty years further on in the world's history, so as to get this wonderful invention in its *perfect* form. It is now in its infancy – the new wonder of the day, just as I remember Photography was about 1850.'

The Royal Engineers had already formed a balloon section, and the first powered aeroplane flight was only thirteen years off when he made that note, but he never seems to have speculated about powered flight, in spite of the time and space theme which recurs in his think-

Three portraits by Carroll: Bishop
Wilberforce ('Soapy Sam'), his
friend Robert Faussett, and his
younger brother Wilfred astride an
early bicycle.

ing and writing. When he was only seventeen he wrote *A Hemispherical Problem*: 'Supposing on Tuesday, it is morning at London; in another hour it would be Tuesday morning at the west of England; if the whole world were land we might go on tracing Tuesday morning, Tuesday morning all the way round, till in twenty-four hours we get to London again. But we *know* that at London twenty-four hours after Tuesday morning it is Wednesday morning. Where, then, in its passage round the earth, does the day change its name?' And that notion was crystallized in Alice's run with the Red Queen, who explained: ' . . . it takes all the running *you* can do, to keep in the same place. If you want to get somewhere else, you must run at least twice as fast.'

As an Oxford undergraduate Charles worked hard for exams and fed the appetite for knowledge which was so characteristic of his generation. That he was not too much of a swot to take at least a conventional interest in sporting events is revealed at the tail end of a letter to his cousin Frank: 'I am afraid you will hardly get here in time to see any of our boat-races, as Saturday week will be the last night of them: we have not made a bump yet, but have very fair hopes of doing so before they are over.'

During the whole of his life at Oxford he kept himself physically fit by much walking. That he could still enjoy a fairly hazardous 'scramble' at the age of twenty-two shows that his studies had not made him just a creature of the midnight oil. From Whitby, where he had joined a party to work through the long vacation of 1854, he wrote to his sister, describing a trip to Goathland:

Preparing for Eights Week: though no athlete, Carroll loyally kept abreast of University sporting events.

Whitby, Yorks: Carroll's first seaside inspiration.

The road down to the cascade consisted of mud & water, with a preponderance of the latter, so I was rash enough to set the example of returning up the side of the cliff, instead of by the road. Only one of the men followed at first, & he did so, thinking the ascent would be easy: a little earth, he says, came crumbling down upon him, but he thought I was throwing it down in fun. However when my cap came flying down upon him, & at the same moment he received a clod of earth in each eye, he began to think more seriously of it. At that precise moment both my feet had lost hold at once, & if the root I was hanging to had broken I must have come down, & probably carried him with me. . . . Just at the top it was hardest of all; it was only to be done by crawling up through the mud, holding by 2 roots, without whose help it would have been impossible. My companion took 5 minutes longer, & subsequently 4 other men reached the top, all covered with mud.

The Whitby cramming party, originally facetiously proposed as '25 hours' *hard* work a day', was effective in gaining him a First in the Final Mathematics School, followed by his BA at the end of the year which also marked the close of his time as an undergraduate. Whitby also produced his first published pieces. A poem in the *Whitby Gazette* called 'The Lady of the Ladle' described:

> *A very heavy swell indeed,*
> *Men thought him, as he swaggered by,*
> *Some scion of nobility,*
> *And never dreamed, so cold his look,*
> *That he had loved – and loved a Cook.*

In the *Whitby Gazette* he also wrote a story, 'Wilhelm von Schmitz' which, in between its long-winded periods and local allusions, had good moments: ' . . . wafted on the landward breeze, came an aroma, dimly suggestive of salt herring, and all things from the heaving waters in the harbour to the light smoke that floated gracefully above the housetops, suggested nought but poetry. . . . ' One of his Whitby companions, Dr Thomas Fowler, caused a literary flutter after Charles's death in 1898 by declaring that Alice was 'incubated' there: 'Dodgson used to sit on a rock on the beach, telling stories to a circle of eager young listeners of both sexes.' This, as we shall see, does not agree with the river idyll which Lewis Carroll himself claimed as the genesis of the story. Nevertheless, he seems to have found himself as a story-teller, a poet, a pedlar of magic – outside his own family circle. The touchstone was childhood.

THE FOLLOWING YEAR of 1855, the first to be documented, at least in part, by his diary entries, was significant for Charles Lutwidge Dodgson. It saw him established as a teacher of mathematics, installed for keeps within the shelter of Christ Church. The Crimean War gets two brief mentions in the journal. That Black Sea coast was remote indeed from the sunny flow of academic and cultural life through the diary pages. In March he was sent some copied-out lines 'on the Balaklava charge' and commented, 'I do not believe that Tennyson could ever have written such lines as:

> *For up came an order, which*
> *Someone had blundered –*

or talked about sabres "sab'ring". If genuine, they are very unworthy of him.'

Tennyson, who had succeeded Wordsworth as Poet Laureate five years before, had lost no time in composing 'The Charge of the Light Brigade', which had been published in the *Examiner* only a couple of months after the disastrous engagement. People made copies and passed them round. When in August 1855 Charles received Tenny-son's *Maud*, in which the 'Charge' first appeared in book form, he noted: 'He has improved . . . the "Balaclava Charge" very much; the "some one had blundered" has disappeared, but the sabres are still "sabring".' He did not think Tennyson's volume as a whole would 'either raise or lower his reputation'. This cool assessment did not inhibit his pursuit of Tennyson as a celebrity for his camera two years later.

Charles was reading much poetry and no doubt cultivating the ear which was to serve him so well – and a very acute ear it was, delighting in parody and pastiche. Nearly all his memorable verse is based on the work of other poets. In that creative year of 1855 he was parodying Thomas Moore:

> *I never nurs'd a dear gazelle*
> *To glad me with its soft black eye . . .*

The first two verses of Carroll's version went:

> I never loved a dear Gazelle –
> *Nor anything that cost me much:*
> *High prices profit those who sell,*
> *But why should I be fond of such?*

> To glad me with his soft black eye
> *My son comes trotting home from school;*
> *He's had a fight but can't tell why –*
> *He always was a little fool!*

Diary references to poets studied and appreciated by Charles while in his twenties show remarkable omissions. Shakespeare is a strong presence but Elizabethan, Jacobean, Augustan voices seem to be mute.

He was already managing well enough in this golden year. For the Croft *Mischmasch* magazine he wrote verses headed thus:

Stanza of Anglo Saxon Poetry:

> TWAS BRYLLYG, AND THE SLYTHY TOVES
> DID GYRE AND GYMBLE IN THE WABE:
> ALL MIMSY WERE THE BOROGOVES;
> AND THE MOME RATHS OUTGRABE.

He then added learned notes such as:

BRYLLYG (derived from the verb to BRYL or BROIL), 'the time of broiling dinner, i.e. the close of the afternoon.'
SLYTHY (compounded of SLIMY and LITHE). 'Smooth and active.'
TOVE. A species of Badger. They had smooth white hair, long hind legs, and short horns like a stag; lived chiefly on cheese.

With this first spark of the inspired fantasy, still home and even nursery oriented, the diary reveals that the bookish Charles was not turning his back upon the sports or pleasures of the adult world. On 16 February: 'My second essay in learning skating. I very soon got a severe fall, cutting open my forehead, by hurrying too precipitately: this stopped the day's performance.'

On 21 June ' . . . paid a long visit to the Royal Academy, and then went on to Lords' [*sic*], where I stayed to the end of the 1st innings of Cambridge (139), and to see Oxford in.' Afterwards at Covent Garden he found *The Barber of Seville* 'all the more tedious to me as I knew hardly any of the music'.

There were two events in that June of 1855 which affected the course of his life – his confrontation with live theatre, and the arrival in Oxford of a little girl called Alice.

At the theatre he saw Shakespeare, often given in bits according to the custom of the time. Yet he attended so much ephemeral rubbish that it seems likely that he rarely if ever enjoyed a good play. His enthusiasm which, begun with the toy theatricals and dressing-up of the Croft nursery, was to prevent him, as we shall see, from becoming a full minister of the Anglican Church, burst forth in a diary entry of 22 June 1855, describing a visit to the Princess's Theatre in Oxford Street, then under the management of Charles Kean:

The evening began with a capital farce *Away with Melancholy*. And then came the great play *Henry VIII*, the greatest theatrical treat I ever had or expect to have – I had no idea that anything so superb as the scenery and dresses was ever to be seen on the stage. Kean was magnificent as Cardinal Wolsey, Mrs Kean a worthy successor to Mrs Siddons in Queen Catherine, and all the accessories without exception were good – But oh, that exquisite vision of Queen Catherine! I almost held my breath to watch; the illusion is perfect, and I felt as if in a dream all the time it lasted. It was like a delicious reverie, or the most beautiful poetry. This is the true end and object of acting – to raise the mind above itself, and out of its petty everyday cares – never shall

Carroll's first and most treasured experience of the theatre: Queen Catherine's dream from *Henry VIII*, elaborately rendered by Charles Kean at the Princess's Theatre, Oxford St.

Opposite, transfixed by an umbrella: one of Carroll's original illustrations for 'The Three Voices', a parody of Tennyson. Later acquaintance with the Laureate never developed into friendship.

I forget that wonderful evening, that exquisite vision – sunbeams broke in through the roof and gradually revealed two angel forms, floating in front of the carved work on the ceiling: the column of sunbeams shone down upon the sleeping queen, and gradually down it floated a troop of angelic forms, transparent, and carrying palm branches in their hands: they waved these over the sleeping queen, with oh! such a sad and solemn grace. So could I fancy (if the thought be not profane) would real angels seem to our mortal vision.

Earlier that month the old dean of Christ Church had died, and was replaced by Henry George Liddell, best known to posterity for his compilation with Robert Scott of the Greek-English lexicon. Liddell had been domestic chaplain to the Prince Consort and head-master of Westminster School, and was to reign at Christ Church for thirty-six years. 'In most people the Dean inspired awe,' wrote a contemporary. '. . . He hated humbug. He disliked shyness in others, although he was the shyest of men himself.' This formidable and strikingly handsome cleric brought with him an equally formidable and handsome wife and four children – Harry aged eight, the eldest, and three daughters, the middle one being Alice, aged three when Charles Dodgson in his twenty-third year first set eyes on her, the creature who was to become the touchstone of his genius.

To mark the arrival of a new dean, Charles Dodgson was made a 'Master of the House'. This gave him all the privileges of a Master of Arts within Christ Church precincts. Like many Victorians, including such men as I. K. Brunel, Charles liked to end his diary year on a note of self-assessment: 'I am sitting alone in my bedroom this last night of the old year, waiting for midnight. It has been the most eventful year of my life: I began it a poor bachelor student, with no definite plans or expectations; I end it a master and tutor in Ch. Ch., with an income of more than £300 a year, and the course of mathematical tuition marked out by God's providence for at least some years to come. Great mercies, great failings, time lost, talents misapplied – such has been the past year.'

Less than a year later he was complaining (to himself or to posterity, who knows?), 'I am weary of lecturing, and discouraged. I examined six or eight men today who are going in for Little-Go, and hardly one is really fit to go in. It is thankless, uphill work, goading unwilling men to learning they have no taste for, to the inevitable neglect of others who really want to get on.'

Certainly he soon wearied of undergraduates. They were rated collectively as a necessary chore, not noticed as individuals – or photo-graphed. His lack of curiosity towards people not of his own choosing extended to the college servants, who waited on him hand and foot for nearly half a century. His was a kind and gentle nature, but he

Henry Liddell, eminent Victorian, dean of Christ Church, and part-author of the famous Greek-English lexicon. Alice was just three years old in 1855 when the Liddells arrived at Oxford.

took them all for granted as part of the lower orders who 'knew their place'.

He in turn wearied undergraduates. Sir Herbert Maxwell re-collected, in 1932, 'the singularly dry and perfunctory manner in which he imparted instruction to us, never betraying the slightest personal interest in matters that were of deep concern to us.' Another witness, H. F. Howard, wrote: 'In dealing with us undergraduates, he never smiled or shewed the smallest sign of his pent-up humour.'

Nor was he cut out for teaching boys. To test himself on this score he arranged, on 29 January 1856, to take classes at St Aldates School: 'I gave the first lesson there to-day, to a class of eight boys, and found it much more pleasant than I expected. . . .'

Only ten days later: 'The school class noisy and inattentive – the novelty of the thing is wearing off, and I find them rather unmanageable.'

A little over two weeks later: 'Class again noisy and inattentive – it is very disheartening and I almost think I had better give up teaching there for the present.'

Three days after that: 'Left word at the school that I shall not be able to come again for the present. I doubt if I shall try again next term....'

He continued to teach undergraduates because it was his duty. He avoided professional and social contacts with small boys – unless, like Henry Liddell, they had attractive sisters.

In the midst of the sad failure with the boys of St Aldates, the name Lewis Carroll was created. Charles at the age of twenty-four had been transferring his talents as parodist, humorist and versifier from domestic magazines towards professional journals. He consistently failed to get into *Punch*, but he contributed to a short-lived periodical called (and he criticized the choice of title) the *Comic Times*. When this failed the editorial staff started a monthly called *The Train*. The

'What I look like when I'm lecturing.' Carroll's shyness and stammer usually prevented any rapport with the breezy young men of mid-Victorian Oxford (*right*).

'The Artful Dodger', an 1858 costume portrait by Carroll of Quintin F. Twiss, one of the few undergraduates he found sympathetic.

editor continued to be Edmund Yates, a prolific journalist who, like Trollope, held an appointment in the Post Office for most of his working life. When Charles submitted his poem 'Solitude', signed 'BB' (no one has ever discovered why), Yates asked for a proper *nom de plume*. Charles tried Dares – after his birthplace. Yates said this was 'too much like a newspaper signature'. So, on 11 February 1856, Charles Dodgson presented his renowned *alter ego* in rather doubtful company thus:

Wrote to Mr Yates sending him a choice of names:
1 *Edgar Cuthwellis* (made by transposition out of 'Charles Lutwidge').
2 *Edgar U. C. Westhill* (ditto). 3 *Louis Carroll* (derived from Lutwidge . . . Ludovic . . . Louis, and Charles). 4 *Lewis Carroll* (ditto).

Yates made his choice, saving Alice and posterity from Edgar Cuthwellis, and Dodgson welcomed his pseudonym with the terse diary entry on 1 March, *'Lewis Carroll* was chosen'.

One of the earliest works to carry the new signature was 'The Path of Roses', an excruciating poem on Florence Nightingale:

> *Not as in rest she bowed,*
> *But large hot tears were coursing down her cheek,*
> *And her low-panted sobs broke awefully*
> *Upon the sleeping echoes of the night.*

Lewis Carroll, as we may now call him, had already begun to accept that his own drawings were not quite good enough for

'Hiawatha's Photographing' (1857) details the extreme complication of early photography – 'Mystic, awful was the process.' *Below*, a self-portrait with the MacDonald children (1863). Having set up the picture, Carroll arranged for an assistant to uncap the lens.

publication – there had been several editorial rejections. Nevertheless he was not content that Yates was to publish 'The Path of Roses' in *The Train*, but insisted on suggesting 'a subject for an illustration, basing it on the concluding lines of the poem. The lady standing near the window where the sun's last rays are streaming in: at the other side the vision of the hospital-scene fading into the darkness, and already so faint that the furniture etc. behind are beginning to be visible through it.' Charles Bennett, the illustrator, in this case did as he was told.

Lewis Carroll went on drawing, but he really excelled as a photographer, and has been described as the best photographer of children in the nineteenth century. The origin of this interest is recorded in a diary entry of 22 January 1856: 'Wrote to Uncle Skeffington to get me a photographic apparatus, as I want some other occupation here, than mere reading and writing.' On 18 March he went with Reginald Southey, a Christ Church colleague already established as an amateur photographer, to choose apparatus from T. Ottiwell of Charlotte Street, off the Caledonian Road. 'The camera with lens etc will come to just about £15,' he wrote at the time, and later that year he declared: 'It is my one recreation and I think it should be done well.' This sizeable sum by no means completed the outfit. It would include numerous bottles, dishes, glass plates, glass measures and funnels,

Tom Taylor, dramatist, critic, and editor of *Punch*. Through Taylor Carroll became friends with a wide circle, including the actress Ellen Terry and her family.

and a portable dark tent or cupboard. This was supported on a tripod stand, and could be folded up for transport. The time Lewis Carroll must have spent packing up this outfit – knowing his fastidiousness in packing his personal belongings, wrapping each item separately in paper twice its own bulk – hardly bears thinking of.

Carroll used to send his equipment by rail in advance when he travelled. In London he managed to stuff it all in a cab, and established his studio for short spells wherever he could scrounge an agreeable set which was also accessible to his sitters. Through acquaintance with the archbishop he was able to use Lambeth Palace. He also took a fancy to D. G. Rossetti's garden, and may have overstayed his welcome. He descended on Tom Taylor, editor of *Punch*, at 8.30 a.m.: 'I had the cellar as a darkroom and the conservatory as a studio, and succeeded in getting some very good portraits.'

From May 1856 to July 1880 he pursued photography so intensely that it is difficult to imagine how he fitted in his industrious career

An early photographic glass-house:

First, a piece of glass he coated
With collodion, and plunged it
In a bath of lunar caustic . . .

Opposite, Carroll's Oxford home
for thirty years. This elegant suite
was located in the right-hand
corner of the picture of Tom Quad.

as a don and created *Alice*, together with unflagging literary and mathematical miscellanea. At first he took his photographs at Christ Church in his own rooms or in the Deanery, occasionally hiring a studio outside. When in 1868 he moved into his splendid suite of rooms, now partly converted into a Common Room, in the north-west corner of Tom Quad, he obtained permission to erect a photo-graphic glass house on the roof. One of the many children he photo-graphed there, Evelyn Hatch, could 'remember climbing up the dark oak staircase leading out of Tom Quad to the studio on the top floor of his rooms. The smell of certain chemicals will still bring back a vision of the mysterious dark cupboard where he developed his plates, of the dressing-room where strange costumes had to be donned, and of the rather awe-inspiring ceremony of being posed, with fastidious care. . . .'

Alice Liddell, the original Alice, told her son in after years: 'Much more exciting than being photographed was being allowed to go into the darkroom and watch him develop the large glass plates.'

To quote Alice Liddell in this connection is to anticipate events. The camera with all its paraphernalia may well have been the un-wieldy vehicle of his first approach to Alice, but in the year he bought it, his first full year as a 'master and tutor in Ch. Ch.' (his most cherished abbreviation), there were at least two more events of significance for him.

The first was the physical shock of catching an epileptic resident of the college as he fell in a fit. 'I am thankful that I was passing at the moment,' he wrote, 'and so had the opportunity of being of use in an emergency. I felt at the moment how helpless ignorance makes one, and I shall make a point of reading some book on the subject of emergencies, a thing that I think everyone should do.' He began by ordering *Hints for Emergencies*, which became the foundation of a comprehensive library of medical books of which, wrote Colling-wood, 'no doctor need have been ashamed'. By special bequest in his will it went to his nephew Bertram Collingwood, who became professor of physiology at St Mary's, Paddington, where a Lewis Carroll children's ward was opened in the 1930s. Anatomy, physio-logy and pathology were all subjects that fed Charles Dodgson's appetite for knowledge. He also tested his nerve by attending an operation at Bart's Hospital – an amputation of a leg above the knee, lasting more than an hour. 'This is an experiment I have long been anxious to make in order to know whether I might rely on myself to be of any use in cases of emergency, and I am very glad to believe that I might.' His medical knowledge was effortlessly and accurately applied to the creatures of his imagination. And in *Sylvie and Bruno* he wrote: 'One needn't be a *Doctor* to take an interest in medical books.'

The second significant event of that year was his reading of Charles Kingsley's first novel, *Alton Locke*: 'It tells the tale well of the privations and miseries of the poor, but I wish he would propose some more definite remedy, and especially that he would tell us what he wishes to substitute for the inquitous "sweating" system in tailoring and other trades. If the book were but a little more definite, it might stir up many fellow-workers in the same good field of social improvement. Oh that God, in His good providence, may make me hereafter such a worker! But, alas, what are the means?'

Then he went on, 'How few seem to care for the only subjects of real interest in life. – What am I, to say so? Am I a deep philosopher, or a great genius? I think neither. What talents I have, I desire to devote to His service, and may He purify me, and take away my pride and selfishness. Oh that I might hear "Well done, good and faithful servant"!' Just over a week later he was at the theatre, and wrote a much more lengthy diary entry describing 'five hours of unmixed enjoyment' which included Kean as Hamlet, 'really wonderful performing dogs', and a 'dumb show entirely by children . . . the prettiest thing I ever saw on the stage'.

Heaven forbid that Carroll should be made out to be frivolous, though he loved fun; or to be insensitive, for most people who knew him said he was kind. Yet apart from that cry, 'What are the means?' and his vow to serve the Almighty, he did little to bring the social problems of his time within the dimensions of his world. He was born and brought up in the industrial north, yet he was not interested in working conditions. When his prayer to be involved in the struggle against the sweating systems, in which children worked till they dropped, was recorded in his diary, he was meeting the first of his always genteel child friends. Thus he dedicated himself to his own brand of unrelenting work and well organized pleasure, the comfortable unreal world from which poverty, ugliness, and social problems were excluded almost as rigorously as ungodly thoughts.

THE TAKING OF holy orders went with the job, but was also a natural desire for a devout son of the parsonage, with an inherited sense of duty to the Anglican Church. The approach to ordination was not easy. Collingwood, with the advantage of having seen diary entries of the period which subsequently disappeared, wrote that Charles Dodgson 'was not prepared to live the life of almost puritanical strictness which was then considered essential for a clergyman and he saw that the impediment of speech from which he suffered would greatly interfere with the proper performance of his clerical duties.' There was the additional discomfort that Dr Wilberforce, the bishop of Oxford, had declared that a 'resolution to attend theatres or operas was an absolute disqualification for Holy Orders.'

Fortunately he learnt that the bishop's stricture applied only to fully ordained priests, not to deacons. But he did not mention this issue, which must have influenced him quite strongly, when many years later he described his situation to a godson:

When I reached the age for taking Deacon's Orders, I found myself established as the Mathematical Lecturer, & with no sort of inclination to give it up & take parochial work: & I had grave doubts whether it would not be my duty *not* to take Orders. I took advice on this point (Bp Wilberforce was one that I applied to), & came to the conclusion that, so far from educational work (even Mathematics) being unfit occupation for a clergyman, it was distinctly a *good* thing that many of our educators should be men in Holy Orders. And a further doubt occurred – and I could not feel sure that I should ever wish to take *Priest*'s Orders. . . . So I took Deacon's Orders in that spirit. And now, for several reasons, I have given up all idea of taking full Orders, & regard myself (tho' occasionally doing small clerical acts, such as helping at the Holy Communion) as practically a layman.

Even as an ordained deacon Dodgson had to comply with the other main condition of Studentship, which was celibacy. A Student who married forfeited his job, but was usually presented with one of the Christ Church livings. The likelihood of Charles marrying and settling down in a country parish, as his father had done, had always been envisaged by the family. He himself did not rule it out. Replying during this period to his father's suggestion for a system of saving and insurance, he wrote: 'If at any future period I contemplate marriage (of which I see no present likelihood), it will be quite time enough to begin paying the premium. . . . '

When he was thirty-nine Dodgson wrote: 'A working life is a happy one, but oh that mine were better and nearer to God.' Derek Hudson shrewdly caps that with the comment: 'It was preferable that Lewis Carroll should have been a busy bachelor than an unhappy husband.'

The disappearance of his diaries for 1858 to 1862, after they were seen by Collingwood, has aroused the suspicion that they contained clues either to religious doubts during the period of his ordination or to an unhappy love affair, and were therefore destroyed by his sisters. Nothing has been found to substantiate either theory – and not for want of looking.

After his ordination in 1861, Charles struggled courageously with his stammer. Throughout his clerical life he occasionally took services and preached sermons, always speaking slowly, and noting on one occasion in his diary 'the two words "strife, strengthened", coming together were too much for me.'

Settling into the secure and sheltered microcosm of Victorian Christ Church for the rest of his life, he was indeed a prodigiously busy bachelor. His commitment as a teacher was heavy. He was also working at literary and poetic journalism, and such sidelines as puzzles. At the same time he was beginning to produce mathematical works, his first book being *A Syllabus of Plane Algebraical Geometry*, published in 1860. For the next forty years his veritable lust for print and paper went unabated. Poetry, mathematics, children's fantasies, logic, puzzles, university ephemera, made up the flood of publications which requires a 300 page catalogue – *The Lewis Carroll Handbook* – compiled originally by Sidney Herbert Williams and Falconer Madan in the 1930s and augmented and reissued in the 1960s by Roger Lancelyn Green, editor of *The Diaries*. Many of the works so devotedly cherished are quite unacceptable to posterity, and were not particularly popular in their own time. Except for specialist readers few of them merit shelf space, and indeed, but for *Alice* and the *Snark*, they would long since have vanished in the extensive Victorian literary limbo.

No wonder Dodgson's lights habitually burned on into the small hours as he obsessively filled sheets of paper – the right size for the right purpose – with violet and black ink, and sometimes in his latter years with typescript. For twenty-four years many of his daylight hours were taken up with photography, not only the camera work but the processing, and with the search for sitters and subjects. Described by Mark Twain, after their only meeting, as 'the stillest and shyest full-grown man I have ever met except Uncle Remus', Lewis Carroll as a photographer was aggressive, often socially inept, sometimes insensitive to the domestic upheavals he caused. He was unremitting in his pursuit of his two specialities – famous people and (attractive) children. The results which have survived certainly justify the pains he took.

He tried hard for Queen Victoria through intermediaries, but without success. His direct approach to the Prince of Wales, on the other hand, makes saddening reading. The Prince (Edward VII to be) had returned from North America and was completing his education as an undergraduate of sorts attached to Christ Church. Queen Victoria suddenly arrived in December 1860 and toured the college. In the evening there was an entertainment at the Deanery. Carroll's part in it seems to have been embarrassing: 'I found an opportunity of reminding General Bruce of his promise to introduce me to the Prince, which he did at the next break in the conversation H.R.H. was holding with Mrs Fellowes. He shook hands very graciously, and I began with a sort of apology for having been so importunate about the photograph. He said something of the weather being against it, and I asked if the Americans had victimised him much as a sitter; he said they had, but he did not think they had succeeded well, and I told him of the new American process of taking twelve thousand

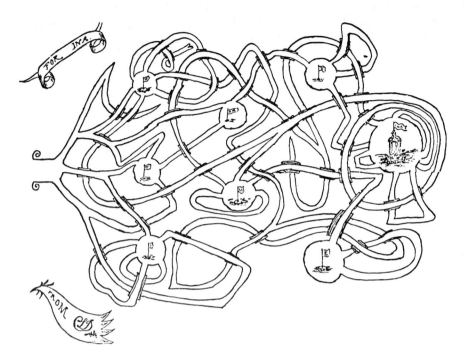

photographs in an hour. Edith Liddell coming by at the moment, I remarked on the beautiful *tableau* that the children might make: he assented, and also said, in answer to my question, that he had seen and admired my photographs of them. I then said I hoped, as I had missed the photograph, he would at least give me his autograph in my album, which he promised to do. Thinking I had better bring the talk to an end, I concluded by saying that, if he would like copies of any of my photographs, I should feel honoured by his accepting them, he thanked me for this, and I then drew back as he did not seem inclined to pursue the conversation.'

Though the Prince had had enough of it, photography was still an exciting and fashionable novelty. Lewis Carroll, like his great contemporary photographic portraitist Julia Margaret Cameron, was uninfluenced by the set pieces of the professionals. Mrs Cameron regarded photography as a 'divine art'. She had the faculty, Gernsheim suggests, 'of piercing through the outward appearance to the very soul of the individual'. He judges Carroll more 'a master of composition'.

One of Carroll's keener sought objectives outside Oxford was the Poet Laureate Alfred Tennyson, the celebrity of the age. So in 1857, on his way back from his only visit to Scotland, he 'happened' to find himself in the Lake District, and indeed at Coniston where the Tennysons were staying. He made up his mind to 'take the liberty of calling'. The great man was out but Carroll made himself agreeable

Puzzle-making was a pastime Carroll shared with his child friends. This labyrinth, drawn for Ina Watson, leads through the letters of her sisters' names – Hartie and Mary – to her own name on the final flag.

Tennyson and his son Hallam, taken at Coniston in 1857. Carroll mastered his shyness in order to seek out celebrities as photographic subjects.

to Mrs Tennyson and to the two sons, 'the most beautiful boys of their age I ever saw', whom he arranged to photograph a few days later.

On his next visit, 'the door opened, and a strange shaggy-looking man entered: his hair, moustache and beard looked wild and neglected: these very much hid the character of the face. He was dressed in a loosely fitting morning coat, common grey flannel waist-coat and trousers, and a carelessly tied black silk neckerchief. His hair is black: I think the eyes too; they are keen and restless – nose *acquiline* [*sic*] – forehead high and broad – both face and head are fine and manly. His manner was kind and friendly from the first: there is a dry lurking humour in his style of talking.'

This first encounter was successful enough. Carroll flatteringly asked the meaning of various passages in *Maud*. Tennyson said he would have liked to take up photography, but dreaded the amount of patience required. He agreed to sit for Carroll, and duly emerged rather swarthily for posterity.

The relationship did not end there. Two years later Carroll turned up at the Isle of Wight when Tennyson was at Farringford. He was at pains to explain in a letter to his cousin William that someone had 'basely misrepresented me if he said that I followed the Laureate down to his retreat'. He added: 'Being there, I had the unalienable right of a free-born Briton to make a morning call.' Then – horror! – he was not recognized. 'There was a man painting the garden railings when I walked up to the house, of whom I asked if Mr Tennyson were at home, fully expecting the answer "No", so that it was an agreeable surprise when he said, "He's there, sir," and pointed him out, and, behold! he was not many yards off, mowing his lawn in a wide awake and spectacles. I had to introduce myself, as he is too short-sighted to recognize people, and when he finished the bit of mowing he was at. . . . '

Carroll was invited back that evening and noted that 'the beautiful little Hallam [his son] remembered me, more readily than his father had done'. He refused Tennyson's offer of a pipe to smoke, and surprisingly approved of the great man's statement that 'clergymen as a body didn't do half the good they might if they were less stuck-up and showed a little more sympathy with their people'.

That Tennyson thought of the young don primarily as a photographer was apparent when he spoke of 'dreaming' long passages of poetry, then turned to Carroll and said, 'You, I suppose, dream photographs?' Six years later, in 1865, Carroll gave the Poet Laureate (though the acquaintanceship had not ripened) a copy of *Alice in Wonderland*, which could have established him in Tennyson's eyes as something more than a man with a camera. Alas, a sadly discreditable situation developed. Carroll, by then well established, wrote in 1870:

Ventnor, Isle of Wight. Carroll's attempt to renew his acquaintance with the Tennysons led to the rumour that he had 'followed the Laureate down to his retreat' at Farringford.

Dear Mr Tennyson,

It is so long since I have had any communication with your family that you will have almost forgotten my name by this time, I fear. I write on a matter very similar to what I have written about to you on two previous occasions. My deep admiration for your writings (extending itself to your earlier poems as well) must be my excuse for thus troubling you.

There is a certain unpublished poem of yours, called 'The Window', which it seems was printed for private circulation only. However it has been transcribed, and is probably in many hands in the form of M.S. A friend, who had had a M.S. copy given to him, has in his turn presented me with one. I have not even read it yet, & shall do so with much greater pleasure when I know that you do not object to my possessing it. What I plead for is, first, that you will make me comfortable in possessing this copy by giving your consent to my preserving it – secondly, the further permission to *show* it to my friends. I can hardly go so far as ask for leave to give away copies of it to friends, tho' I should esteem such a permission as a great favour.

Some while ago, as you may remember, I had a copy lent me of your 'Lover's Life' – & a young lady, a cousin of mine, took a M.S. copy of it. I wrote to you about it, & in accordance with your wish prevailed on her (very reluctantly, I need hardly say) to destroy the M.S. I am not aware of any other copies of *that* poem in circulation – but *this* seems to me a different case. M.S. copies of 'The Window' are already in circulation, & this fact is unaffected by my possessing, or not possessing, a copy for my own enjoyment. Hoping you will kindly say you do not object to my – first reading – & secondly preserving the M.S. that has been given me, & with kind remembrances to Mrs Tenny‑son & your sons.

  I remain,
    Very truly yours
     C. L. Dodgson.

Tennyson had not cleared these works for publication and his wife wrote back:

Dear Sir,

It is useless troubling Mr Tennyson with a request which will only revive the annoyance he has already had on the subject & add to it.

No doubt the 'Window' is circulated by means of the same unscrupulous person whose breach of confidence placed 'The Lover's Tale' in your hands.

It would be well that whatever may be done by such people a gentleman should understand that when an author does not give his works to the public he has his own reasons for it.

  Yours truly,
    Emily Tennyson.

Carroll, with enough years of academic cut and thrust behind him, did not take that lying down. His reply, addressed to Mr, not Mrs, Tennyson, was moderate enough but predictably rose to the taunt in the final sentence which 'certainly implies, however unintentionally, a belief that I have done something ungentlemanly. Let me then remind you that in all these matters I have been a purely passive agent, & that in all cases I have consulted your wishes & scrupulously followed them. It is by no act of mine that this poem is now in circulation, & that a copy of it has come into my hands. Under these circumstances I may fairly ask you to point out what I have failed to do that the most chivalrous sense of honour could require.'

The Tennysons wrote at least once more, not making matters much better. Then Carroll sent off this letter:

My Dear Sir,
Thus it is, as it seems to me, that you first do a man an injury, and then forgive him – that you first tread on his toes, & then beg him not to cry out!

Nevertheless I accept what you say, as being in substance, what it certainly is not in form, a retraction (though without a shadow of apology or expression of regret) of all dishonourable charges against me, & an admission that you had made them on insufficient grounds.

Sincerely yours
C. L. Dodgson.

This correspondence, brought to light by Derek Hudson, shows Carroll at his most tetchy, and Tennyson as one of those not much taken with the drolleries of *Wonderland*, and still regarding its creator as the over-persistent young don called Dodgson with the photographic apparatus.

That apparatus was active in many other directions. The diary plotted it all: 'Oct. 1 1863. Mr Rossetti proposed getting Robert Browning to come on Wednesday to be photographed. Celebrities seem to come like misfortunes – "it never rains but it pours."' Browning never arrived but, on 6 October, 'Went over to Mr Rossetti's, and began unpacking the camera, etc. While I was doing so Miss Christina Rossetti arrived, and Mr Rossetti introduced me to her. She seemed a little shy at first, and I had very little time for conversation with her, but I much liked the little I saw of her. She sat for two pictures, Mr Rossetti for one. . . . '

In November of that year he took the Crown Prince of Denmark, whom he described (not without pique), as 'evidently a much brighter specimen of royalty than his brother-in-law' – the Prince of Wales whose refusal to be photographed still rankled. The following year a small accolade came, somewhat deviously, from the Queen herself: 'Heard from Mrs Read, enclosing a letter from Lady A. Stanley [wife of the dean of Westminster] to Lady A. M. Dawson in which she says that she has shown my photographs to the Queen, and is commanded to say that "Her Majesty admires them very much. They are such as the Prince would have appreciated very highly and taken much pleasure in".' What the Prince Consort

Naturalism was the quality which Carroll, a passionate photographer for twenty-four years (1856–1880), brought to the new art. The portrait of Frederick, Crown Prince of Denmark – taken when he was a Christ Church undergraduate – is formal but not stiff, while the studies of the Millais family (with Effie in the centre), and of two of his aunts, are agreeably relaxed.

'Coates', a daughter of one of the Croft employees (1857), was the subject for one of Carroll's rare pictures of working-class children. The natural setting marks a radical departure from the elaborate compositions of most contemporary photographers.

missed, and posterity has gained, is an arresting portrait gallery of Carroll's friends and relatives, Oxford academics, Pre-Raphaelites, miscellaneous celebrities – and above all, children, the well-nourished children of the well-to-do, from whom came the delectable Alice.

FROM A WINDOW of the library at Christ Church they will show you how you can look down over the lawn and flower beds of the Deanery, as did Charles Dodgson as sub-librarian in that elevated place. On an April day in 1856 he went into the garden with a friend to photo-graph the cathedral: 'The three little girls were in the garden most of the time, and we became excellent friends: we tried to group them in the foreground of the picture, but they were not patient sitters. I mark this day with a stone.'

This mark occurring occasionally in the diaries was for exceptional people or especially significant events. Even this, his first meeting with Alice Liddell, hit home in some way – and it was not the photo-graphs which were significant for they did not come out. He was in love. Alice was the first and greatest of these love affairs with maidens, unformed women, little girls of nursery age, creatures in whose

Lewis Carroll in middle age.

presence he lost his stammer, smelled the breeze across the cornfields of Daresbury and found the reality of Wonderland. His love life was as simple as that. He adored the image substantiated first in Alice Liddell, then in a succession, sometimes a plurality, of other child friends. This was the precious reality of his life, right up to its ascetic, overworked end at the age of sixty-six.

Where was the orgasm? Was there an orgasm? In his introduction to his *Pillow Problems* (seventy-two problems, chiefly in algebra, plane geometry or trigonometry) he wrote of nocturnal 'unholy thoughts, which torture with their hateful presence the fancy that would fain be pure'. Apart from this unsensational hint there is nothing in his writing, behaviour, or the witness of those who knew him, that his well-cared-for if sometimes underfed body reached any climax of lust. This is not so very odd. Many die virgins. Many live with a love image without sexual desire. The man was unique in that the image provoked such poetic fantasies as *Alice* and the *Snark*. The man was also warm-blooded enough to enjoy the physical and tactile kiss-hug-cuddle of pre-pubescent girlhood. He was not deprived. He was prodigiously self-indulgent and always had what he wanted. Suggestions that he was a pervert or a 'dirty old man' using child photography to further his carnal desires are as absurd as the fashionable theories that he was an acid head who climbed into Wonderland by way of the Caterpillar's mushroom. He was a singularly happy and contented man who enjoyed good health with a touch of hypochondria. Some have rated him epileptic, others have questioned his mental balance. All fail to prove their theories or to add much to the treasures of Wonderland. To a little girl who took his fancy his heart was open and communication was fully and easy.

The Caterpillar on a mushroom, smoking: Carroll's own illustration. The hallucinogenic quality of Alice's experiences has given a contemporary twist to the continuing fascination of the story.

To the world at large he was a kindly man, quizzical, pedantic, extra alert because of his deafness and, as he got older, somewhat querulous and withdrawn. About his child friendships he was never secretive, indeed always explicit. He was totally self-centred. He knew, and got, what he wanted. He expected them to end with the end of childhood:

'About nine out of ten, I think, of my child-friendships got ship-wrecked at the critical point "where the stream and the river meet", and the child-friends, once so affectionate, became uninteresting acquaintances, whom I have no wish to see again.'

The intensity of his feeling for Alice Liddell steeply declined after the publication of the book, and quite evaporated after her marriage to Reginald Hargreaves, a county cricketer, crack shot and landowner. Twenty-three years after that Golden Afternoon he could write without even addressing her as Alice:

My dear Mrs. Hargreaves, – I fancy this will come to you almost like a voice from the dead, after so many years of silence, and yet those years have made no difference that I can perceive in *my* clearness of memory of the days when we *did* correspond. I am getting to feel what an old man's failing memory is as to recent events and new friends, (for instance, I made friends, only a few weeks ago, with a very nice little maid of about twelve, and had a walk with her – and now I can't recall either of her names!), but my mental picture is as vivid as ever of one who was, through so many years, my ideal child-friend. I have had scores of child-friends since your time, but they have been quite a different thing.

However, I did not begin this letter to say all *that*. What I want to ask is, Would you have any objection to the original MS. book of 'Alice's Adventures' (which I suppose you still possess) being published in facsimile?

Alice grown up. Carroll lost touch
with his 'ideal child friend' before
she became Mrs Reginald
Hargreaves, and recorded his
astonishment at being offered the
chance to photograph her in 1870.
Above, the same subject, taken by
his great contemporary Julia
Margaret Cameron in 1872, shows
the difference between the two
photographers. Cameron preferred
close-ups, while Carroll found
full-length portraits more expressive.

So romance faded into exquisite donnish politeness.

In entertaining and photographing child friends Carroll was well acquainted with the menace of Mrs Grundy. He wrote to his illus-trator Harry Furniss: 'I wish I could dispense with all costume, naked children are so perfectly pure and lovely, but "Mrs Grundy" would be furious. . . .'

His attitudes had to be modified, but they continued, and it is difficult to believe that any monster of lust was concealed in the coy explicitness of this letter written two years before his death to Mrs Aubrey-Moore:

You and your children seem so well disposed to regard me as a friend (though a *little* too much inclined to treat me as a 'lion' – a position I cordially detest) that I should like to try, if I may, to know them better. Child-friends *will* grow up so quick! And most of mine are now grown up, though by no means ceasing to be 'child-friends'. But my life is *very* busy, and is nearing its end, and I have *very* little time to give to the sweet relief of girl-society. So I have to limit myself to those whose society can be had in the only way in which such society is worth having, viz., one by one.

Would you kindly tell me if I may reckon *your* girls as invitable (*not* 'inevitable'?), to tea, or dinner, *singly*. I know of cases where they are invitable in *sets* only (like the circulating-library novels), and such friendships I don't think worth going on with. I don't think anyone knows what girl-nature *is*, who has only seen them in the presence of their mothers or sisters.

Also, are they kissable? I hope you won't be shocked at the question, but nearly all my girl-friends (of all ages, and even married ones!) are now on those terms with me (who am now sixty four). With girls under fourteen, I don't think it necessary to ask the question: but I guess Margery to be *over* fourteen, and, in such cases, with new friends, I usually ask the mother's leave. . . .

By that time he had had more than forty years of coping with Mrs Grundy, with anxious mamas and, not least, with the conventions of Oxford life. Though his Christ Church appointment was celibate, he was a presentable and indeed eligible young don when he started his cultivation of Alice and her family. In May 1857, when he had just met William Makepeace Thackeray at breakfast and found him 'simple and unaffected', his diary suddenly assumed an apprehensive tone:

Took Harry Liddell to chapel, and afterwards walked back with the children to the Deanery. I find to my great surprise that my notice of them is construed by some men into attentions to the governess, Miss Prickett. . . . Though for my own part I should give little importance to the existence of so groundless a rumour, it would be inconsiderate to the governess to give any further occasion for remarks of the sort. For this reason I shall avoid taking any public notice of the children in future, unless any occasion should arise when such an interpretation is impossible.

Miss Prickett herself may have winced at this notoriety or welcomed it – for she had her worldly side; she ended her life as proprietress of the Mitre Hotel, Oxford.

Despite the governess scare, Carroll was soon back on intimate terms with the Liddell children, always under the baleful eye of their mother, who at a later stage was to tear up his letters to Alice. The Golden Afternoon illuminated the period and, beside inspiring the poetry, set the pattern of the long years of unbroken child adoration. Reinforcements were carefully selected, now and then unsuccessfully. A setback was suffered with 'a quite new little friend, Lily Alice Godfrey, from New York: aged eight; but talked like a girl of sixteen, and declined to be kissed on wishing goodbye, on the ground that she "never kissed gentlemen". It is rather painful to see the lovely simplicity of childhood so soon rubbed off: but I fear it is true that there are no children in America.'

Did he ever pause to consider 'the lovely simplicity of childhood' in industrial Britain, in the North of his upbringing, or in the other end of the London where he took his pleasures? Between the Golden Afternoon and the publication of *Alice in Wonderland*, children who were not clean and kissable were providing evidence for three com‚ missioners appointed by Parliament to enquire into 'The Employ‚ ment of Children and Young Persons in Trades and Manufacturers not already regulated by law'. Ann Elizabeth Powell, aged twelve, stated:

Carrying bricks is my regular work, but today I am 'drawing' a kiln. Get 6d a day. Have an hour for dinner, and eat it here. . . .

Went to a red‚brick yard near, at 10 years old. . . . From 6 to 6 was the regular time. . . . My work was carrying bricks and heaving clay. I carried enough clay for four bricks on my head, and for two in my arms. My head used to ache, but not my back.

Was at a day school a little bit. Father reads the Bible out, but he only comes home once a week. An angel is very pretty. I wished I was an angel. They live in heaven. I hope I shall be one some day, and sit in Jesus' lap.

The commissioner reported that Ann 'struck me by the earnest way in which she was doing her share of a work which certainly is heavy for a child, as a slight calculation shows. The kiln, containing 17,000 bricks, of $7\frac{1}{4}$ lbs each when dry, was to be emptied by ten persons in a day and a half; i.e. this girl had to catch and toss on to her neighbour in a day of only the usual length a weight of more than 36 tons, and in so doing to make backwards and forwards 11,333 com‚ plete half turns of her body, while raised from the ground on a sloping plank. The plank is said not to be needed all the time. When called down by me she was panting.'

The working children of Birmingham in the 1860s were remote indeed from the God-fearing education-orientated world of Lewis Carroll and his little friends. The official report quotes one of them as having 'heard about Jesus Christ, but it's so long since that I've forgot.' Another declared, 'I would know a primrose, it's a red rose like:' and another didn't 'know what a river is, or where the fishes are. . . .'

Carroll chose to ignore the news that must have trickled through about these other children, though Tennyson might cry:

> *Is it well that while we range with Science, glorying in the time,*
> *City children soak and blacken soul and sense in city slime?*

Even Oxford was only as sheltered as one chose to make it. A contemporary, the Professor of Poetry 1857–67, was Matthew Arnold, who wrote: 'Our inequality materializes our upper class, vulgarizes our middle class, brutalizes our lower class. . . .' But Carroll knew his place: 'At Margate I made very many pleasant acquaintances, chiefly on account of being attracted by their children: very few turned out to be above the commercial class – the one drawback of Margate society.'

THE REVD C. L. DODGSON both enjoyed the fame and also revelled in not enjoying the fame of being Lewis Carroll. He was a great one for having his cake and eating it. Himself a relentless pursuer of celebrities, he rejected a request from *Vanity Fair* for a sitting for a Spy cartoon – 'nothing would be more unpleasant for me than to have my face known to strangers.'

He almost obsessively supervised the illustration, production, and publication of *Alice in Wonderland*, which sold some 110,000 copies in his lifetime. He was enthusiastically committed to the promotion of the *Alice* stories, by cheap, nursery, facsimile editions, by tableaux and operatic adaptation, and by such gimmicks as the Wonderland postage-stamp case. He could, however, be very tetchy about being Carroll. To Edith Rix, a child friend, he wrote: 'Would you tell your mother I was aghast at seeing the address of her letter to me: and I would much prefer "Rev C. L. Dodgson, Ch. Ch., Oxford". When a letter comes addressed "Lewis Carroll, Ch. Ch.", it either goes to the Dead Letter Office, or it impresses on the minds of all letter-carriers, &c., through whose hands it goes, the very fact I least want them to know.' He continued to fulminate about correspondence reaching him addressed Lewis Carroll. Yet to another child friend, Kathleen Eschwege, he subscribed his letter, 'Your affectionate friend, Charles L. Dodgson (*alias* "Lewis Carroll").'

Invented by Carroll in 1888, this 'stamp-case' illustrates his readiness to promote the *Alice* stories commercially.

The Wonderland

Postage-Stamp Case

Carroll's own illustrations to his original manuscript of *Alice* project a softer, dreamier vision than Tenniel's.

In spite of such quixotics he set about his literary affairs with all the thoroughness of a mathematician, and with a promotional flair which would have served him well among the media of this century. The first draft of 18,000 words of *Alice's Adventures Under Ground* was not only lovingly handwritten for the little girl, but was garnished with thirty-seven illustrations by the author. He finished writing in February 1863, but it was not sent to Alice at the Deanery until November 1864. Between those two dates Carroll, from having 'no idea of publication', had by May 1863 been persuaded by various friends to let it be published, and this meant his getting in touch with the Clarendon Press at Oxford to print the work at his expense. But first he made an enlarged draft of 35,000 words, and placed it in the hands of John Tenniel, introduced to him by Tom Taylor, the dramatist and future editor of *Punch*. Tenniel had established himself as a draughtsman with his illustrations to *Aesop's Fables* (1848), the drolleries of which brought him into lifelong association with *Punch*.

When he died in 1914, aged ninety-three, Sir John Tenniel left 2000 *Punch* cartoons – including a biting anti-sweatshop work of 1863, and the famous 'Dropping the Pilot' on the Kaiser's dismissal of Bismarck in 1890. His greatest gift to posterity was the illustrations immortalized in the two *Alice* books. The world has never seen a matching of word with drawing to equal the Carroll/Tenniel

She was a good deal frightened by this very sudden change, but as she did not shrink any further, and had not dropped the top of the mushroom, she did not give up hope yet. There was hardly room to open her mouth, with her chin pressing against her foot, but she did it at last, and managed to bite off a little bit of the top of the mushroom.

*   *   *   *   *

"Come! my head's free at last!" said Alice in a tone of delight, which changed into alarm in another mo- -ment, when she found that her shoulders were nowhere to be seen: she looked down upon an immense length of neck, which seemed to rise like a stalk out of a sea of green leaves that lay far below her.

Tenniel's Duchess was almost certainly inspired by the *Ugly Duchess* of the Flemish painter Quinten Massys (1465–1530), in the National Gallery.

collaboration. For Tenniel it was the least agreeable task in his long life. He took on the first *Alice* book mainly because there were plenty of animals in it and he liked doing animals. Though his own reputation was much enhanced by the *Wonderland*'s success, he refused for a long time to tackle *Through The Looking-Glass*. He was persuaded only by the most urgent entreaties of his tyrannical author to undertake the work. In spite of this, Carroll confided to another illustrator, Harry Furniss, that out of the ninety-two drawings in *Wonderland* he had liked only one. Tenniel was reported by Furniss to have said, 'Dodgson is impossible! You will never put up with that conceited old Don for more than a week!'

Examples of Carroll's notes to Tenniel: 'Don't give Alice so much crinoline', and, 'The White Knight must not have whiskers: he must not be made to look old.' Tenniel sometimes fought back, and sometimes won: 'A wasp in a wig is altogether beyond the appliances of art. . . . Don't think me brutal, but I am bound to say that the "wasp" chapter doesn't interest me in the least, and I can't see my way to a picture. . . . ' Carroll omitted the chapter.

In May 1864 he sent Tenniel the first of the slip (galley) proofs from the Clarendon Press: and Tenniel was already at work when Macmillan agreed to publish the work on a commission basis. This was the beginning of an even more politely abrasive – and profitable – relationship. According to Charles Morgan, in his history of Macmillan's: 'There never was an author more elaborately careful than

John Tenniel (1820–1914), chosen by Carroll to illustrate the *Alice* books, was already well known before achieving lasting fame as a result of them. The little girl Mary Badcock was Carroll's choice of model, accepted by Tenniel, but the features of the White Knight bear a remarkable resemblance to the illustrator's own.

The pantomime at Drury Lane which Carroll attended, with three of the Terry children, on 17 January 1866. 'Little King Pippin', he wrote, 'is the most beautiful spectacle I ever saw in Pantomime.'

Lewis Carroll for the details of production, or one that can have more sorely tried the patience of his publisher.' He bore the expense of his own fussiness and perfectionism, which extended to every aspect of the business. He 'never allowed himself to be far absent from the minds of publisher, printer or binder. . . . Books, ingenuities and trouble poured from him.'

Not even the packers escaped his attention. He sent in a diagram showing how parcels were to be stringed and how the knots were to be tied. This hung for years in the Macmillan post-room. He soon came to regard his publisher also as a general factotum. For many of his frequent forays to London theatres, Macmillan's were given the task of buying his tickets, and making sure that the seats were on the extreme right as he was deaf in his right ear. They were also required to send a 'trusty and resolute messenger' to retrieve watches when he sent them to be mended.

In December 1864, only just after he had given Alice Liddell her manuscript copy (sold in 1928 for £15,400), Carroll sent off to Macmillan 'the whole of my little book in slip. It is the only complete copy I have. . . . I hope you may not think it unfitted to come under your auspices.' If Macmillan's supposed they were dealing with a naïve mathematical cleric they were soon disillusioned. They sent

Carroll a specimen volume in May 1865 which he liked and passed, saying that he wanted publication of the edition of 2000 copies quickly for his young friends, who 'are all grown out of childhood so alarmingly fast'. On 15 July he went to the publisher's office to autograph some twenty copies, and everything was sunny. Five days later he reappeared with gloom in the shape of 'Tenniel's letter about the fairy tale – he is entirely dissatisfied with the printing of the pictures, and I suppose we shall have to do it all again.'

And that is what they did. Carroll declared in his diary that the 2000 copies, for which he had paid the Clarendon Press £135, 'shall be sold as waste paper'. He sent out a circular letter recalling the personal copies he himself had already given away. These – the few survivors have fetched £5000 a piece – were redistributed free to hospitals. The remaining 1,952 unbound sheets were not sold as waste, but shipped to the United States where they were bought, bound and sold by Messrs Appleton of New York – Carroll on this and several other occasions indulging a snobbish contempt for American cultural standards. A new English edition was printed by Richard Clay and published by Macmillan in November 1865. That Tenniel's complaint had been rediculously sensitive, and that Carroll had been absurdly fussy in acting on it, may be gathered from a study of the respective texts in the British Museum.

The book's reception was good, but fell short of acclamation. The *Pall Mall Gazette* called it 'a children's feast and triumph of nonsense'. The *Athenaeum* said, 'This is a dream story, but who can in cold blood manufacture a dream? . . . We fancy that any real child might be more puzzled than enchanted by this stiff, over-wrought story.' Among his appreciative friends, Christina Rossetti thanked him for 'the funny pretty book'.

The book's fame spread by world of mouth, and Lewis Carroll's name, though not the identity of the mathematics don Dodgson, was established as a curiosity in the Victorian scene. There was a new edition each year from 1865 to 1868. In two years he had made a profit of £250 on his original outlay of £350 – which included Tenniel's payment. From 1869 to 1889 there were twenty-six reprintings.

Queen Victoria, widowed four years before the book's appearance, was undoubtedly one of his readers. Walter de la Mare, writing in 1932, quotes an old lady who, at the age of three and a half, and too young to read, had sat on a footstool looking at Tenniel's pictures in the presence of the Queen. 'Noticing this rapt doubled-up little creature in the fire-light so intent over her book, the Queen asked her what it was. She rose and carried it over, and standing at the royal knee opened it at the page where tinied Alice is swimming in the flood of her own tears. . . . This little girl, pointing at the picture, looked up into the Queen's face, and said: "Do you think, please, *you* could cry as much as that?"' The old lady did not remember the Queen's precise reply, though it expressed great enthusiasm for Carroll. It was followed next day by a locket sent from Windsor by special messenger.

There was the story that the Queen had been so pleased with *Alice in Wonderland* that she had asked for the author's next book, and had been sent the *Condensation of Determinants* (1866) or *An Elementary Treatise on Determinants* (1867). The story was so persistent that Carroll, towards the end of his life, printed a denial: 'I take the opportunity of giving what publicity I can to my contradiction of a silly story, which has been going the round of the papers, about my having presented certain books to her Majesty the Queen. It is so constantly repeated, and is such an absolute fiction, that I think it worth while to state, once and for all, that it is utterly false in every particular: nothing even resembling it has ever occurred.'

Despite this the legend persisted, even among Carroll scholars. In 1939 Alexander Wollcott declared: 'Then, when *Alice* was published and won her heart, she [the Queen] graciously suggested that Mr Dodgson dedicate his next book to her. . . . ' He went on to complete the joke as before with the *Determinants*.

'I have . . . a floating idea of writing a sort of sequel,' Carroll informed Macmillan's a few months after the publication of *Wonderland*, while he, as the Revd C. L. Dodgson M A, worked away at the determinants. Once again he envisaged an illustrated book. He did not start writing it until he had tried several artists, and had eventually badgered the reluctant Tenniel into taking it on.

For the *Looking-Glass* there was another Alice. Like the Alice of the Golden Afternoon the significance and circumstances of her appearance were subsequently romanticized. With the mirror-writing of Croft perhaps at the back of his mind, Carroll's 'floating idea' had already taken the direction of a 'visit to Looking-Glass House' mentioned in a letter in December 1867, when he met Alice Theodora Raikes during a visit to his Uncle Skeffington in Onslow Square, London. She lived a few doors away and was the eldest daughter of Henry Cecil Raikes M P, a family friend who became Postmaster-General. She was probably about eight at the time, and played in a communal garden behind the house where Carroll would 'walk up and down, his hands behind him'. And this is how she, who herself became an author, remembered it more than sixty years later:

One day, hearing my name, he called me to him saying, 'So you are another Alice. I'm very fond of Alice. Would you like to come and see something which is rather puzzling?' We followed him into the house which opened, as ours did, upon the garden, into a room full of furniture with a tall mirror standing across one corner.

'Now,' he said, giving me an orange, 'First tell me which hand you have got that in.' 'The right,' I said. 'Now,' he said, 'go and stand before that glass, and tell me which hand the little girl you see there has got it in.' After some perplexed contemplation, I said, 'The left hand.' 'Exactly,' he said, 'and how do you explain that?' I couldn't explain it, but seeing that some solution was expected, I ventured, 'If I was on the other side of the glass, wouldn't the orange still be in my right hand?' I remember his laugh. 'Well done, little Alice,' he said. 'The best answer I've had yet.'

In January 1871 Carroll received from Clay the printers' galley proofs of the complete *Looking-Glass*, and noted, 'The volume has cost me, I think, more trouble than the first, and *ought* to be equal to it in every way.'

The trouble, as usual, was not only his. For most of that year Tenniel was pressed to complete the illustrations. He in turn complained, sometimes successfully, about the text. The publishers had more than their share of troubles too. One of their earlier efforts at a title-page provoked this note:

My title page hasn't had fair play yet – as the printer doesn't follow out my directions. I want the large capitals to have *more below the line than above*: nearly twice as much. In the corrected copy I sent the A & F have slipped a little lower than I meant: the others are about right.

Secondly, the 'AND' ought to be half-way between the two lines, and not (as they have printed it) nearer to the upper line.

Thirdly, the 3 lines of title ought to be closer together, and not so close to the top of the page.

Fourthly, the comma and full-stop ought to be set lower.

'Jabberwocky', which had begun to find its way into print back in 1855, was now enlarged, and demanded very special treatment: 'I want to have 2 pages of "reverse" printing . . . such as you hold up to the looking-glass to read.' He was proposing that the whole of 'Jabberwocky' should be done in mirror-writing of which he himself was a master, as the facsimile of his letter to Edith Ball shows. As we have seen, only the title and the first verse were reverse printed. But with that settled, there was an agonizing fuss over Tenniel's horror picture of the Jabberwock. The extent of this may be judged from the following circular which was actually printed and sent to 'about thirty of his married lady friends,' according to Collingwood:

I am sending you, with this, a print of the proposed frontispiece for *Through the Looking-Glass*. It had been suggested to me that it is too terrible a monster, and likely to alarm nervous and imaginative children; and that at any rate we had better begin the book with a pleasanter subject.

[Mirror-writing letter, reversed]

Nov. 6, 1893.

My dear Edith,
I was very much
pleased to get your nice
little letter: and I hope
you won't mind having
waited rather long. Maud have the Nursery
Alice, won't you have
got the real one. Some
day I will send you the
other book about, called with
"Through the Looking-Glass"
but you had better not have
it just yet, for fear you

Through The Looking-Glass contained a nightmarish quality which Carroll thought might upset his younger readers. In a mirror-writing letter (*left*) to a child friend he promises the book, 'but not just yet', while the Jabberwock illustration (*opposite*) was demoted from the front of the book after a personally conducted audience reaction test.

So I am submitting the question to a number of friends, for which purpose I have had copies of the frontispiece printed off.
We have three courses open to us:
(1) To retain it as the frontispiece.
(2) To transfer it to its proper place in the book, (where the ballad occurs which it is intended to illustrate) and substitute a new frontispiece.
(3) To omit it altogether.
The last-named course would be a great sacrifice of the time and trouble which the picture has cost, and it would be a pity to adopt it unless it is really necessary.
I should be grateful to have your opinion, (tested by exhibiting the picture to any children you think fit,) as to which of these courses is best.

The women and children voted the Jabberwock off the front of the book but not out of it altogether: this unique episode of reader-participation revealed another aspect of Lewis Carroll's pernickety perfectionism – his dedication to his customers.

In December 1871, Macmillan's published 9000 copies of the book and immediately had to order a reprint of another 6000. On 8 December Carroll sent off a hundred free copies, cloth bound, to friends – Tennyson being honoured with one bound in morocco.

He had achieved the unlikely, a second *Alice* book to stand beside the first and to remain always, just in second place in sales, sharing the summit of his achievement. Success was immediate, 'enough to turn a lesser man's head,' Collingwood remarked. Henry Kingsley pontificated: 'I can say with a clear head and conscience that your new book is the finest thing we have had since Martin Chuzzlewit.' The *Athenaeum*, making up for its jibe at *Wonderland*, said it was 'no mere book . . . but the potentiality of happiness for countless children of all ages.'

For Tenniel it was good-bye. 'It is a curious fact,' he wrote later, 'that with *Through the Looking-Glass* the faculty of making drawings for book illustrations departed from me, and, notwithstanding all sorts of tempting inducements, I have done nothing in that direction since.'

The inspiration of the Jabberwock continued to assert itself. *The Hunting of the Snark* was an extension of the subject, set, as Carroll explained, 'in an island frequented by the Jubjub and Bandersnatch – no doubt the very island in which the Jabberwock was slain.'

Surely no poem has even been more analysed. The measure of its quality is that it comes through unscathed, its fun, its magic whole, meaning all things to all men. Just as he had recalled the Golden Afternoon genesis of *Alice*, Carroll now told his admiring public how the *Snark* came about.

'I was walking on a hillside, alone, one bright summer day, when suddenly there came into my head one line of verse – one solitary line – "For the Snark *was* a Boojum, you see." I knew not what it meant, then: I know not what it means, now; but I wrote it down: and, sometime afterwards, the rest of the stanza occurred to me, that being its last line: and so by degrees, at odd moments during the next year or two, the rest of the poem pieced itself together, that being its last stanza.' This celebrated stroll took place in Guildford on a July afternoon in 1874. Pilgrimages have since followed his supposed course. He made a literary myth out of one of those moments of inspiration which happen to every poet at the outset of every poem – though few have made such a meticulous record of the event.

While 'the rest of the poem pieced itself together', Carroll was already deeply into the question of illustration – as always regarded

Opposite, the *Snark*'s illustrations exactly catch the poem's mood. Carroll's ability to pick his illustrators was almost an extension of his own talent.

Henry Holiday, chosen by Carroll to illustrate the *Snark*, was well known for his work on churches. His Boojum (*opposite*) was rejected by the author on the grounds that the creature was unimaginable, and therefore unrepresentable.

by him as a *sine qua non*. His man this time was Henry Holiday, an established painter, sculptor and stained-glass designer (his *Dante and Beatrice* was one of the most reproduced best-sellers of the time), whom he had met four years before when Holiday was in Oxford painting a chapel frieze. In January of the year of the writing of the *Snark*, Carroll called on the artist's family in Hampstead, where Holiday 'showed me the drawings he is doing for me (suggestions for groups of two children – nude studies – for me to try to reproduce in photographs from life) which are quite exquisite.'

The following day: 'Told Holiday of an idea his drawings suggested to me, that he might illustrate a child's book for me. If *only* he can draw grotesques, it would be all I should desire – the grace and beauty of his pictures would quite rival Tenniel, I think.'

When Carroll had written three 'fits' of the *Snark*, according to Holiday he 'asked if I would design three illustrations to them, explaining that the composition would some day be introduced in a book he was contemplating; but as this latter would certainly not be ready for a considerable time, he thought of printing the poem for private circulation in the first instance. While I was making sketches for these illustrations, he sent me a fourth "fit", asking for another drawing; shortly after came a fifth "fit", with a similar request, and this was followed by a sixth, seventh, and eighth. His mind not being occupied with any other book at the time, this theme seemed continually to be suggesting new developments; and having extended the "agony" thus far beyond his original intentions, Mr Dodgson decided to publish it at once as an independent work. . . . '

Holiday 'not unnaturally invented a Boojum', he afterwards explained, and offered it on spec, envisaging it as the *chef-d'œuvre*. Carroll dismissed not only this but any illustration of the Boojum. He told Holiday that all his descriptions of the Boojum were quite unimaginable and he wanted the creature to remain so. He called Holiday's creation 'a delightful monster' but was firm about it being inadmissable. Holiday kept it and subsequently sold it to Falconer Madan, joint editor of *The Lewis Carroll Handbook*. A glance at the drawing may well persuade any reader of the poem that Carroll was right. The incident shows that Carroll, as a true poet, did not wish his work to be interpreted but only illustrated. He was shy of any interpretation of the poem, philosophical, sociological, religious, political. He himself was an intellectual, a mathematician, a puzzle-maker and well equipped to explain, yet he said it was nonsense. All his knowledge, his beliefs, his doubts, contribute to this 'nonsense', his creative reality, his rare – almost his last – moment of inspiration.

The catalyst for this poem was, as before, a child friend, a 'little bare-legged girl in a sailor's jersey who used to run into my lodgings from the sea'. Her name was Gertrude Chataway.

Carroll was at Sandown, Isle of Wight, when Gertrude, almost eight, on holiday with her family, first noticed him:

. . . next door there was an old gentleman – to me at any rate he seemed old – who interested me immensely. He would come on to his balcony, which joined ours, sniffing the sea-air with his head thrown back, and would walk right down the steps on to the beach with his chin in air, drinking in the fresh breezes as if he could never have enough. I do not know why this excited such keen curiosity on my part, but I remember well that whenever I heard his footstep I flew out to see him coming, and when one day he spoke to me my joy was complete.

Thus we made friends, and in a very little while I was as familiar with the interior of his lodgings as with our own.

I had the usual child's love for fairy-tales and marvels, and his power of telling stories naturally fascinated me. We used to sit for hours on the wooden steps which led from our garden on to the beach, whilst he told the most lovely tales that could possibly be imagined, often illustrating the exciting situations with a pencil as he went along.

That summer – another golden summer – Gertrude made such a profound impression that Carroll dedicated *The Hunting of the Snark* to her, writing his acrostic verses within a month of first meeting her:

> *Inscribed to a dear Child:*
> *in memory of golden summer hours*
> *and whispers of a summer sea.*
>
> **G**irt *with a boyish garb for boyish task,*
> **E**ager *she wields her spade: yet loves as well*
> **R**est *on a friendly knee, intent to ask*
> **T***he tale he loves to tell.*
>
> **R**ude *spirits of the seething outer strife,*
> **U**nmeet *to read her pure and simple spright,*
> **D**eem, *if you list, such hours a waste of life*
> **E***mpty of all delight!*
>
> **C**hat *on, sweet Maid, and rescue from annoy*
> **H**earts *that by wiser talk are unbeguiled.*
> **A**h, *happy he who owns that tenderest joy,*
> **T***he heart-love of a child!*
>
> **A**way, *fond thoughts, and vex my soul no more!*
> **W**ork *claims my wakeful nights, my busy days –*
> **A**lbeit *bright memories of that sunlit shore*
> **Y***et haunt my dreaming gaze!*

Gertrude Chataway, Carroll's close companion at Sandown during the summer of the *Snark*, 1875. A drawing by Carroll.

Carroll sent a copy of this to Gertrude's mother, asking her permission to print it. The lady responded favourably, though she had not only overlooked the ingenuity of the double acrostic but had not noticed any acrostic at all. He pointed it out, hoping that it would not affect her permission, adding, 'I shan't tell anyone it is an acrostic – but someone will be sure to find out before long.'

Only a few months before publication, poor Holiday was still having a rough time. His design for the cover of the book was rejected: '*That* would have done beautifully for a volume of poems meant for aesthetic adults,' wrote Carroll to Macmillan's. '*This* book is meant for children.'

Three days later Carroll came up with a gift to the book trade. The book jackets of the period were plain paper wrappers. He gave instructions for the title and author's name to appear on the spine and the front of the wrapper. 'I want you to print it on the paper wrapper,' he instructed Macmillan's. 'The advantage will be that it can stand in bookstalls without being taken out of paper, and so can be kept in cleaner and more saleable condition.' So he 'invented' the modern dust jacket.

He wanted publication of the *Snark* to take place on 1 April 1876: 'Surely that is the fittest day for it to appear?' It came out a few days earlier, and did not excite the critics, though by that time *Alice* was in its forty-ninth thousand and the *Looking-Glass* in its thirty-eighth thousand. On publication day Carroll spent six hours in the Macmillan office inscribing eighty presentation copies. It took all that time, as a number of books for little girls went out with acrostic verse inscriptions. To one of them he wrote: 'When you have read the *Snark*, I hope you will write me a little note and tell me how you like it, and if you can *quite* understand it. Some children are puzzled with it. Of course you know what a Snark is? If you do, please tell *me*: for I haven't an idea what it is like. And tell me which of the pictures you like best.'

He had a sharp eye for seasonal trade. At the start of the following year he wrote to Macmillan's: 'How has the "Snark" sold during the Xmas Season? That, I should think, would be a much better test of its success or failure than any amount of sale at its first coming out. I am entirely puzzled as to whether to consider it a success or a failure. I hear in some quarters of children being fond of it. . . . ' In the next six years it sold 18,000 copies, and by 1908 it had been reprinted seventeen times.

During that year of the *Snark*, 1876, Carroll not only kept up a business correspondence with his publishers but was 'writing a good deal . . . about Logic in algebraical notation', work of slight value on which he expended too much of his later years, for, alas, he was not a great mathematician. Yet his pen danced some skittish measures for Gertrude:

You will be sorry, and surprised, and puzzled, to hear what a queer illness I have had ever since you went. I sent for the doctor, and said, 'Give me some medicine, for I'm tired.' He said, 'Nonsense and stuff! You don't want medicine: go to bed!' I said, 'No; it isn't the sort of tiredness that wants bed. I'm tired in the *face*.' He looked a little grave, and said, 'Oh, it's your *nose* that's tired: a person often talks too much when he thinks he nose a great deal.' I said, 'No; it isn't the nose. Perhaps it's the *hair*.' Then he looked rather grave, and said, '*Now* I understand: you've been playing too many hairs on the piano-forte.' 'No, indeed I haven't!' I said, 'and it isn't exactly the *hair*; it's more about the nose and chin.' Then he looked a good deal graver, and said, 'Have you been walking much on your chin lately?' I said, 'No.' 'Well!' he said, 'it puzzles me very much. Do you think that it's in the lips?' 'Of course!' I said. 'That's exactly what it is!' Then he looked very grave indeed, and said, 'I think you must have been giving too many

kisses.' 'Well,' I said, 'I did give *one* kiss to a baby child, a little friend of
mine.' 'Think again,' he said; 'are you sure it was only *one*?' I thought again,
and said, 'Perhaps it was eleven times.' Then the doctor said, 'You must not
give her *any* more till your lips are quite rested again.' 'But what am I to do?'
I said, 'because you see, I owe her a hundred and eighty-two more.' Then he
looked so grave that the tears ran down his cheeks, and he said, 'You may
send them to her in a box.' Then I remembered a little box that I once bought
at Dover, and thought I would some day give it to *some* little girl or other. So
I have packed them all in it very carefully. Tell me if they come safe, or if
any are lost on the way.

Gertrude was one of the few child friends who remained close on
reaching womanhood – much more so than Alice Liddell. In
December 1891, in his fifty-ninth year, he noted in his diary: 'As
Mrs Hargreaves, the original "Alice", is now at the Deanery, I
invited her . . . over to tea. She could not do this, but very kindly came

over, with Rhoda, for a short time in the afternoon.' By contrast his letter a week or so later to Gertrude began:

'My dear old friend, – (The friendship is old, though the child is young.) I wish a very happy New Year, and many of them, to you and yours; but specially to you, because I know you best and love you most. And I pray to bless you, dear child, in this bright New Year, and many a year to come. . . . '

So in spite of an ever renewed multitude of child friends, and of the tens of thousands more words written, Gertrude kept her magic. There was little poetry or imaginative work of significance after *The Hunting of the Snark*. With this and the two *Alice* books Carroll had found himself in the reality of his genius. With the fame which he quirkily enjoyed went the dismay which every poet has experienced who cannot find a way back to the magic dimension of truth beyond knowledge.

On the three occasions when he stepped right out of himself into that dimension, there was nothing to show that he was treading a path of genius. The works by which all the world knows him spun out of a life regulated by habit, by the routines of work, of entertainment, of the meticulously organized affairs with the never-ending stream of child friends. He was prodigiously involved with life at all levels, but remained within the social and academic structure to which he was confined – or rather, allowed himself to be confined. He was happy – so long as things went his way. 'I don't think he ever laughed,' wrote his former child friend Ethel Rowell, 'though his own particular crooked smile, so whimsical, so tender, so ironic, was in and out all the time.' He was never short of money, and literary prosperity enabled him to be generous in support of his sisters.

Nor was he ever short of creature comforts for the forty-seven years he was at Christ Church, attended by college servants. He kept a note of every menu served to guests in his room, so that no visitor should be confronted with the same meal twice, but he was not himself greedy. Wherever he might be he would only take a biscuit and a glass of wine at luncheon. Hospitality in his quarters was ample enough. On 12 March 1874, for instance, 'we dined a party of eight. . . . The evening went off successfully, I think. We met in the small room, dined in the large room, went back again for dessert, during which the large room was converted into a drawing-room. This seems the best way of using my rooms for a party.' After one such dinner, in May 1871, he announced to Macmillan's that he had invented a table plan which would show guests where to sit, and which gentleman would take in which lady.

Involved in life – and its trivia – as he was, he was also a wholly self-centred man. This did not exclude kindliness and generosity. He just never did anything much that he did not want to do or felt

Opposite, the sheltered world of Oxford: a view through the main gate into Christ Church.

The Soul and the Body.

Dean Liddell and Professor Benjamin Jowett, two of the University's heaviest personalities. Carroll's relations with the Dean, often strained, deteriorated sharply in the 1870s over the issue of Liddell's architectural 'improvements' to the College.

that duty called upon him to do. He contributed fully, and often contentiously, to college life, noting for instance that Michaelmas 1864 was 'a harder-worked term than I have had for a long time.' He had politely abrasive rows with the forceful Dean Liddell. In the 1870s open warfare developed with his denunciation and ridicule of the Dean's alterations and restorations at Christ Church. Carroll aimed three satirical pamphlets at Liddell, and these were duly gloated over by academic society.

While he remained secure in his Life Fellowship, and continued to participate in college affairs, he let his teaching go as *Alice* provided the funds he needed. In 1880 he voluntarily took a cut of £100 in his salary, and the following year gave up his lectureship entirely, piously recording for posterity: 'I shall now have my whole time at my own disposal, and, if God gives me life and continued health and strength, may hope, before my powers fail, to do some worthy work in writing – partly in the cause of Mathematical education, partly in the cause of innocent recreation for children, and partly, I hope (though so utterly unworthy of being allowed to take up such work) in the cause of religious thought. May God bless the new form of life that lies before me, that I may use it according to His holy will!'

He had in fact disliked the job – and the undergraduates. His infrequent references to them in print were usually disparaging. His fame as a writer of fantasy and his fancy for little girls caused some resentment among his contemporaries. He laboured incessantly but failed significantly to further the cause of mathematical education.

Within a year of giving up teaching he took on a job which was acceptably remote from undergraduates, though socially onerous – curator of the Senior Common Room at Christ Church. He accepted this task, not from any high moral principle, but because 'it will take me out of myself a little, and so may be a real good. My life was tending to become too much that of a selfish recluse.'

For a decade he was involved with the college wine-cellar, servants, groceries, fuel and, not least, the moods and behaviour of a 'large and wealthy club', as he once described it. He gave no ground to colleagues, and to servants and catering staff he gave – politely, sometimes even humorously – hell:

'Cauliflowers are *always* sent with no part soft enough to eat except the tops of the flowers. This the Cook defends, & seems to think no one ever expects to eat more: he explains that, if boiled till the stalks are eatable, the flower would be overboiled. All I know is that

Oxford: a view up 'the High' as Carroll saw it.

95

our letters + parcels, a
set of deep
baskets (as more
easily carried
when loaded
than square ones)
with waterproof
covers –
Yours hydrophobically
C L Dodgson

Sketch by Carroll of an improved
design for college messengers'
mailbaskets. As curator of the
Senior Common Room Carroll's
fussiness could be a trial to others.

everywhere, except here, cauliflower is a very nice vegetable, &
eatable as a whole. Here only 5% is eatable, & that absolutely flavour-
less.'

Like the everyday amenities of life, the choice of company or of
solitude was much enhanced by bachelorhood: 'While undressing,
thought of a process (which I worked out next day) for finding
angles from different sines and cosines,' he jotted in November 1875,
recording a typically undistracted nocturne. But, calamity in 1891!
An invasion of his privacy drove him to send this note to the college
steward: 'On Saturday morning, just after I had got out of bed, a
ladder was reared against the bedroom window, & a man came up to
clean it. As I object to performing my toilet with a man at the window,
I sent him down again, telling him "you are not to clean it *now*,"
meaning, of course, that *that* window was to be left till I was dressed.
Instead of moving away the ladder to the next windows (my smaller
sitting-room) they went away, and have not returned. So the bedroom-
window, the 2 windows of the sitting room, & the window of the
pantry, are not yet cleaned. They are ready to be cleaned at any time,

whether I am here or not, with the single exception that I object to to the bed-room window being cleaned while I am dressing.'

To a contemporary, Professor York Powell, Lewis Carroll said that he found the days too short. This witness, like many others, remarked on Carroll's immense capacity for work, and also noted appreciatively:

... his kindly sympathies, his rigid rule of his own life, his unselfish love of the little ones, whose liegeman he was, his dutiful discharge of every obligation that was in the slightest degree incumbent on him, his patience with his younger colleagues, who were sometimes a little ignorant and impatient of the conditions under which alone Common-room life must be in the long run ruled, his rare modesty, and the natural kindness which preserved him from the faintest shadow of conceit, and made him singularly courteous to every one, high or low, he came across in his quiet academic life, – these his less-known characteristics will only remain in the memories of his colleagues and contemporaries. Dodgson and Liddon long made the House Common-room a resort where the weary brain-worker found harmless mirth and keen but kindly wit.

The kitchens at Christ Church. Although himself uninterested in food, Carroll nagged the staff relentlessly to improve culinary standards at the College.

Dr Henry Liddon, Carroll's companion on his only venture abroad, to Russia (1867).

Opposite, the seaside, where Carroll went every summer for most of his life, provided a variety of little girls to be entertained and sketched. Eastbourne was his choice for the last twenty years: 'When the people get weary of life,' he wrote, 'they rush off to the seaside, to see what bathing-machines will do for them.'

Henry Liddon, later canon of St Paul's, was a lifelong friend and colleague. In one particular, however, he did not see eye to eye with Carroll: 'I have never been inside a theatre since I took Orders,' he declared, ' . . . and I do not mean to go into one, please God, while I live.' With this good man, Carroll at the age of thirty-five set out on his sole trip abroad. ' . . . we have decided on Moscow! Ambitious for one who has never yet left England,' he wrote in July 1867.

Their excursion lasted two months. Carroll wept at the beauty of Cologne Cathedral, found a Dresden girls' playground 'a very tempting field for a photographic camera', and in Russia assisted Liddon in carrying out an unofficial goodwill mission between Anglicanism and Russian Orthodoxy. Both men kept diaries. Carroll's deepest feeling was recorded on the way back, standing in the prow of the cross-Channel steamer for a first glimpse of Dover, 'as if the old land were opening its arms to receive its homeward bound children.' The trip seems to have left little lasting impression on him. He barely referred to it in after years.

He moved about, but never very far, usually within a pattern dictated by habit and the university year, and always packing a Bradshaw, his name meanwhile travelling all over the world.

In 1868 he passed through the Great Northern Railway station at Croft for the last time. His father had died suddenly the year before, and after twenty-five years the family left the Rectory. Charles took on the full responsibility as head of the family, and installed his six unmarried sisters in a substantial red-brick house, 'The Chestnuts', at Guildford, which became a fixed point in his movement pattern. For the rest of his life he regarded this as his family home, always spent Christmas there, and there, tended by his sisters, died.

His summer vacations drew him to the seaside, never to enter the water, but to write, to take long walks, and above all to cultivate little girls. From 1873 to 1876 he went to Sandown, Isle of Wight. His much longer attachment, from 1877 till his death, was to Eastbourne. On 31 July 1877 he noted: 'Moved to my new lodging, 7 Lushington Rd, where I have a nice little first floor sitting room with a balcony, and bedroom adjoining. Mr and Mrs Dyer keep the lodging: he is at the post office here.' For twenty summers he lodged there, and moved with the Dyers when they took another house, further from the sea, two years before he died. His visits are recalled in a plaque outside the semi-detached Lushington Road property, and by a curious bed-table desk made for him by a member of the Dyer family, and now in the possession of one of their descendants.

Whenever he travelled by train or walked by the sea, Carroll carried puzzles for the instant amusement of little girls, and on the beach he armed himself with pins to assist the little things to hold up their sometimes voluminous garments when they paddled. He always

Celebrities and children, Carroll's two main photographic themes, were combined in studies of the painter Arthur Hughes and his daughter Agnes (*right*), and the writer George MacDonald with Lily MacDonald (*opposite*).

took care to establish himself socially with parents and guardians. Shortly after his arrival at the Dyers' he noted: 'It seems that I could if I liked, make friends with a new set of nice children every day! This morning I have added to my list a Mr Hull (of the Temple), wife and family (4 girls, Alice, Agnes, Eveline, and Jessie). . . .'

A 'list' was not just a figure of speech. This forty-five-year-old cleric, working on a pamphlet about Euclid, solemnly entered in his diary for 27 September 1877: 'My child friends, during this seaside visit, have been far more numerous than in any former year. I add a list: WADDY, Minnie, Loui, Edith, Annie and Lucy; DYMES, Margie, Ruth, Dora, Helen, Maud; CHRISTIE, Dora; BLAKEMORE, Edith; WOODERUFFE, Violet; BURTON, Mabel; GORDON, Emily, Violet; WHICHER, Rose; HULL, Alice, Agnes, Eveline and Jessie;

BELL, Grace, Maud, Nellie; SMITH, Agnes, Gracilla. Besides these were others. . . . '

Though the charming, whimsical and celebrated man undoubtedly gave pleasure and provided treats and much innocent fun and frolic for all these and more, they had been carefully culled by him for their looks, their youthful zest and their social acceptability. His own gratification was the driving force. He would even speak of borrowing children from their parents. Not surprisingly his activities led to talk: 'Dear May Miller was engaged to dine with me: but Mrs Miller wrote to say there was so much "ill natured gossip" afloat, she would rather I did not invite either girl without the other.'

Nobody but an obsessively self-centred man, chaste though he was, could have demanded such a massive diet of youth and gone to such lengths to sustain it. Its promiscuity within social limits, and its persistence till the end of his life, might be compared with that of Don Juan himself. The first years of his life at Daresbury, the formative years at Croft, the essences of childhood and youth, were perpetuated even in his mid-sixties as a reality innocent and wonderful – a reality he had to have and made sure that he got.

He worked it all out, referred to himself as a 'lonely bachelor', and from time to time something rather more than superficial would develop. The Agnes Hull met and catalogued at Eastbourne became 'My Darling Aggie' and received letters like this: 'Oh yes, I know quite well what you're saying – "Why can'n't the man take a *hint*? He might have *seen* that the beginning of my last letter was meant to show that my affection was cooling down!" Why, of course I saw it! But is that any reason why *mine* should cool down, to match? I put it to you as a reasonable young person – one who, from always arguing with Alice [Aggie's sister] for an hour before getting up, has had good practice in Logic – haven't I a right to be affectionate if I like? Surely, just as much as *you* have to be unaffectionate as *you* like. And of course you mustn't think of *writing* a bit more than you *feel*: no, no,

Barefoot on the beach: two child friends sketched by Carroll at Sandown in the summer of 1874.

truth above all things! (Cheers – Ten minutes allowed for refresh⁄ment.) I came up to town on Monday with Mr Sampson (some of you have met him at Eastbourne) to see "The Cup" & "The Belle's Stratagem", & on Tuesday I made a call or two before going back to Guildford, & passed "High St. Kensington". I had turned it (half) over in (half of) my mind, the idea of calling at 55. But Com⁄mon Sense said "No. Aggie will only tease you by offering you the extremity of her left ear to kiss, & will say, 'This is for the *last* time, Mr Dodgson, because I'm going to be sixteen next month!' Don't you know", said Common Sense, "That *last times* of anything are very unpleasant? Better avoid it, & wait until her sixteenth birthday is over: then you'll be on shaking⁄hand terms, which will be calm & comfortable." "You are right, Common Sense," said I, "I'll go & call on other young ladies . . .'"

The lady most often canvassed as Lewis Carroll's one great though unfulfilled love affair – by those who insist that he must have had one – has been the ravishing Victorian actress Ellen Terry. He was twenty⁄four and she was eight years old, making her stage début, when he first saw her and judged her 'a beautiful little creature'. Seven years later he was hoping that Tom Taylor could introduce him to Ellen and her sister Kate – 'I must try to get them as sitters'. He was not alone in his admiration. The painter G. F. Watts not only painted

A Carroll study of 'Xie' Kitchin, daughter of one of his oldest friends. To achieve excellence in photography, Carroll said, one needed only to 'take a lens and put Xie before it'.

Ellen Terry, famous actress and perceptive friend of Carroll for much of his life, wrote: 'He was as fond of me as he could be of anyone over the age of ten.' *Above*, at her stage début in 1856, aged eight, when Carroll first saw her. *Above right*, a portrait by her first husband, G. F. Watts (1864). *Right*, as a 'perfect' Ophelia in 1879.

them – his famous painting *The Sisters* – but swept Ellen into matrimony. She was fifteen, Watts was forty-five when they married in 1864. The marriage soon broke down, though they were not divorced till 1877.

Carroll admired the 'beautiful head by Watts of Mrs Watts' at the Royal Academy in 1868: and at the end of that year met 'to my delight, the one I have always most wished to meet of the family, Mrs Watts'. He had by that time made himself familiar with the Terry family at their Stanhope Street home in the hope of photographing the sisters. After this first encounter he went on record that she was 'lively and pleasant, almost childish in her fun, but perfectly ladylike'. Had she not been 'ladylike' the affair would have ended there. For the next three years, however, he saw her often in and out of the theatre, even cajoled her into playing a croquet game of his own invention, and reading his play *Morning Clouds*, which deservedly never darkened any stage. She was sufficiently unmoved by such attentions to elope in 1868 with E. W. Godwin, architect and theatrical designer. She remained with him in exile from London for six years, and bore him a son who became celebrated as Gordon Craig.

A family of actors: the Terrys photographed by Carroll in 1865.

This unconventional behaviour did not deter Carroll from admitting his admiration of her – on stage. But not until her 'simply perfect' Ophelia in 1879 did he renew the acquaintance off stage. Then he found her as 'charming as ever' married again with two children. His last sight of her was at Winchelsea two years before his death, when she had sent a carriage to meet him and his current child friend Dolly Rivington – 'Miss Terry and Dolly were swinging, side by side in hammocks'. She treated him with affection at all times, and shrewdly wrote of him in her autobiography: 'He was as fond of me as he could be of anyone over the age of ten.'

If sustained adult passion passed him by, he was at least fortunate in being always able to attract and hold the interest of children. And children were of course the inspiration for his most creative work, both in literary and in photographic terms. But in July 1880 Carroll renounced photography, suddenly and for ever.

The reasons for this decision are still not entirely clear. It has been suggested that his dislike of the 'new' dry-point process may have been responsible, but neither this nor the pressures of authorship seem sufficient to account for the giving up of a lifelong passion.

A few scattered records point to emotional reasons. There had been an awkward incident early that year involving the daughter of a fellow don, Sidney James Owen. Carroll, mistaking her age (which was seventeen), had given 'Atty' Owen a kiss on parting, and this had been badly received by her mother. Carroll was forty-eight; and enough of a ripple of gossip went out to disquiet him. 'Maybe he realized that there might be some subconscious impropriety involved,' Roger Lancelyn Green, the editor of *The Diaries*, has suggested:

The popularity of dry plate photography, which by 1880 had largely superseded the more sensitive process used by Carroll, coincided with, but did not account for, his renunciation of the medium.

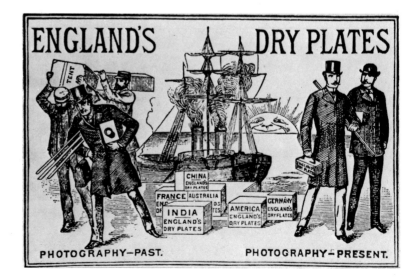

Nude children, *left*, by Sutcliffe and, *below*, by Robert Faulkner, were an acceptable subject for Victorian photographers, but Carroll's growing involvement with the theme may have played some part in his decision to give up photography in 1880.

'Certainly, it seems, he felt that, whether as a mortification or as a safeguard, photography must be given up. But he was deeply hurt by the insinuation, and a friend of that period tells me that he "dropped" a great many of his Oxford friends and their families – in her case for a matter of nearly ten years.'

Another school of thought connects the cessation of Carroll's photography with his interest in photographing little girls in the nude. But this was by no means a new preoccupation. In May 1867 he had noted: 'Mrs L. brought Beatrice, and I took a photograph of the two; and several of Beatrice alone, "sans habilement".' Towards the end of his photographic career he recorded the visit of two little Oxford girls to his studio: 'I had warned Mrs ** that I thought the children so nervous I would not even ask for "bare feet" and was agreeably surprised to find they were ready for any amount of undress, and seemed delighted at being allowed to run about naked. It was a great privilege to have such a model as ** to take: a *very* pretty face, and a good figure.'

In the summer of 1879 he wrote: 'Brought Annie and Frances (and their mother) in a cab, and did some more photos of them in the same dress as before (i.e. their "favourite dress of 'nothing'").' He wrote of the nude studies as the 'kind of photograph I have often done lately'.

In the last three decades of Victoria's reign, photographs of children in the nude, and voluptuously fleshy paintings of naked adults, were not only acceptable but fashionable. Carroll's portraits 'sans habilement' were neither a novelty nor necessarily an outrage. What seems likely is that he pulled himself up because he realized that this aspect of his hobby was becoming obsessive and, for a bachelor don, socially dangerous. So he abandoned photography altogether. At his death the existing nude studies were returned, according to his will, to the families of the subjects.

His candid appreciation of undressed little girls – and its hazards – continued. Some years later he wrote on the subject of book illustrations to Harry Furniss, 'I wish I dared dispense with all costume, naked children are so perfectly pure and lovely, but "Mrs Grundy" would be furious, – it would never do. . . . You must remember that the work has to be seen, not only by children, but by their *Mothers*: and some *Mothers* are *awfully* particular. . . .'

Mothers might be particular, but when it came to recruiting child friends this man of God could himself be very particular indeed. A former child friend, Beatrice Hatch, was engaged in social work in Oxford in 1894 when Carroll met her with some of the girls in her charge. Clearly it was not any aspect of social work which concerned him: only himself, his craving and – heaven help him! – his status, when he wrote to Beatrice:

I should like to know, for curiosity, who that sweet-looking girl was, aged 12, with a red nightcap. I think she had a younger sister, also with a red nightcap. She was speaking to you when I came up to wish you good-night. I fear I must be content with her *name* only: the social gulf between us is probably too wide for it to be wise to make *friends*. Some of my little *actress*-friends are of a *rather* lower status than myself. But, below a certain line, it is hardly wise to let a girl have a "gentleman" friend – even one of 62!

Always affectionately

yours, C.L.D.

During his twenty-four years of active photography the camera provided this shy, stammering man with a positive weapon of social aggression. It was never more successfully deployed than in the capture of the 3rd Marquess of Salisbury, a future prime minister who succeeded Lord Derby as Chancellor of Oxford University in June 1870. At his installation ceremony Carroll's Russian travelling companion, Liddon, was being given an honorary D.C.L., and through him Carroll approached Lady Salisbury with a request to photograph the children. This was successful – thanks perhaps to *Alice*. 'I fancy "Wonderland" had a great deal to do with my gracious reception,' he gloated in his diary.

The day after his introduction the Salisbury family converged on Carroll's rooms. First Salisbury, himself a Christ Church man, was photographed in his robes as Chancellor, then with his sons. In the afternoon Lady Salisbury came back with the children, and they all admired Tenniel's new drawings for the *Looking-Glass*. Then Lady Salisbury 'went away to make calls, leaving me the children'. He photographed the girls, Lady Maud and Lady Gwendolen, and

Maud and Gwendolen Cecil,
photographed by Carroll in 1870,
and their father the Marquess of
Salisbury. A self-caricature (*below*)
represents Carroll as having had his
head turned by his grand new
acquaintance.

also the four children together. Thus began an acquaintanceship
which lasted, not without its ups and downs, for over a quarter of a
century. It was never a profound relationship. Lady Salisbury
enjoyed the company of the celebrated author of *Alice*. Lord Salisbury,
outside politics, was interested in mathematics and theology, and
himself contributed copiously to the *Quarterly Review*. He liked to
entertain a man with whom he had interests in common. The children
liked him too. A month after his first encounter, when he was staying
in London, he recorded that 'the four Cecils rode over and spent
$\frac{1}{2}$ hour with me – nominally to bring the wire-puzzle I had given to
Gwendolen'.

The following winter he was invited twice to stay at Hatfield
House, and could not go, though he kept up a correspondence with
the two girls. In the summer of 1871 he obtained Lady Salisbury's
permission to take them to the Royal Academy. Then, on 1 July, he
'left King's Cross by the midnight train, and found a brougham

waiting for me at Hatfield station, and reached the house in a few minutes: none of the family visible.' The reason for the nocturnal journey seems to have been that he had been spending that Saturday evening witnessing an open air drama entitled *Snowdrop*, acted by children. The Salisburys were by this time railway-oriented, having created the main drive to connect the station directly to the House.

This was the first of seven visits, sometimes to coincide with 'Gwennie's' birthday in the summer, and more often for the New Year parties. In June 1889 Carroll described the cosy, socially exalted scene to his adored and adoring child friend Isa Bowman, who had played the part of Alice on the stage the year before:

> . . . there is the Duchess of Albany here, with two such sweet little children. She is the widow of Prince Leopold [The Queen's youngest son], so her children are a Prince and Princess: the girl is 'Alice', but I don't know the boy's Christian name: they call him 'Albany', because he is the Duke of Albany. Now that I have made friends with a real live little Princess, I don't intend ever to *speak* to any more children that haven't any titles. In fact, I'm so proud, and I hold my chin so high, that I shouldn't even *see* you if we met! No, darling, you mustn't believe *that*. If I made friends with a *dozen* Princesses, I would love you better than all of them together, even if I had them all rolled up into a sort of child-roly-poly. . . .

During nearly every visit he told stories about Sylvie and Bruno to the assembled children. But he rebelled at the idea that this was a duty. On one New Year occasion he 'declined to undertake my usual role of storyteller in the morning, and so (I hope) broke the rule of being always expected to do it.' He went on with Sylvie and Bruno stories, however, choosing his own time. His correspondence and acquaintanceship with the girls continued after Maud had married and become the Countess of Selborne. Lord Salisbury was an apparently uncomplaining target for notions, suggestions, requests for patronage and pamphlets. The Carroll bombardment included his pamphlet on vivisection, a prospectus for a school of dramatic art, papers on electoral reform, a proposal for a series of firewatch stations on tall London buildings such as St Paul's, a suggestion that the government might introduce Bills into either House for debate and then send them to the other House for passing into law.

For the problems of Home Rule for Ireland Carroll offered, in a six-page letter, the simple solution that Lord Salisbury should dispatch Queen Victoria to Ireland to show herself to the people. Salisbury courteously replied, even after he became prime minister, to all the Carroll communications, however bizarre. He found time for an interview when Carroll launched a campaign for the evacuation of the inhabitants of the island of Tristan da Cunha. Carroll's interest in this stemmed from his youngest brother, the Revd Edwin

'Bruno's Revenge': Carroll's original sketch, printed in *Aunt Judy's Magazine*, December 1867. The story formed part of *Sylvie and Bruno*, published at the close of 1889.

Heron Dodgson, having elected to serve as chaplain on the island. 'I cannot think he will find this an object worthy to devote much of his life to – with so many thousands in equal need in England,' Carroll has written in 1881 when his brother went out. The notion of moving the population, then about a hundred, out of the island arose from the departure of the whaling trade from the area, leaving the islanders on the verge of starvation. Carroll wrote a number of letters to Salisbury between 1885 and 1887, and had a meeting ('not

Cartoon of Carroll by Harry Furniss, his illustrator for *Sylvie and Bruno*.

very fruitful, I fear') with the prime minister in 1885. The evacuation campaign failed, but the islanders received relief and survived, their numbers more than doubled a century later.

If the impact of Carroll upon the Cecils was socially agreeable though not deep, a strong whiff of the style and environment of Hat-field House permeated his last massive imaginative work, *Sylvie and Bruno* (1889), and *Sylvie and Bruno Concluded* (1893), each containing 'nearly as much as the two "Alice" books put together', as Carroll pointed out in the advertisements.

For Harry Furniss, who did forty-six illustrations for each book, the collaboration was a sort of calculated risk, a challenge for which he devised a strategy: 'No artist is more matter-of-fact or businesslike than myself: To Carroll I was not Hy. F., but someone else, as *he*

Coping with Carroll was a problem for all his illustrators. Here Furniss drew an episode in which he simulated an eccentricity to match Carroll's own.

was someone else. I was wilful and erratic, bordering on insanity. We therefore got on splendidly.' He made no bones about the text being 'a bitter disappointment to me. I did not want to illustrate a book of his with any "purpose" other than the purpose of delightful amusement, as Alice was.'

He had been warned by Tenniel to expect detail, and this is how it came to him from Carroll: 'As to your Sylvie I am charmed with your idea of dressing her in *white*; it exactly fits my own idea of her; I want her to be a sort of embodiment of Purity. So I think that, in Society, she should be wholly in white – white frock ("clinging" certainly; I *hate* crinoline fashion): also I *think* we might venture on making her *fairy* dress transparent. Don't you think we might face Mrs. Grundy to *that* extent? In fact I think Mrs G. would be fairly content at finding her *dressed*, and would not mind whether the material was silk, or muslin, or even gauze. One thing more. *Please* don't give Sylvie high heels! They are an abomination to me.'

Furniss clowned along outrageously. He assumed eccentricities to match those of Carroll, which were very real, and included an obsession about secrecy. No one was to see the text. So at one time Carroll cut it into horizontal strips of four or five lines, shook them in a sack then pasted them up as they happened to come out. They were then given a series of numbers which, as Furniss said, 'would really have turned my assumed eccentricity into positive madness'. So he sent back the manuscript, went on strike, and won that round.

His *tour de force* was an occasion when he had finished none of the drawings:

Lewis Carroll came to dine, and afterwards to see a batch of work. He ate little, drank little, but enjoyed a few glasses of sherry, his favourite wine. 'Now,' he said, 'for the studio!' I rose and led the way. My wife sat in astonishment. She knew I had nothing to show. Through the drawing-room, down the steps of the conservatory to the door of my studio. My hand is on the handle. Through excitement Lewis Carroll stammers worse than ever. Now to see the work for his great book! I pause, turn my back to the closed door, and thus address the astonished Don: 'Mr Dodgson, I am *very* eccentric – I cannot help it! Let me explain to you clearly, before you enter my studio, that my eccentricity sometimes takes a violent form. If I, in showing my work, discover in your face the slightest sign that you are not *absolutely* satisfied with any particle of this work in progress, the *whole* of it goes into the fire! It is a risk: will you accept it, or will you wait till I have the drawings *quite* finished and send them to Oxford?'

'I-I-I ap-preciate your feeling – I-I-should feel the same myself. I am off to Oxford!' and he went.

When Furniss's work was done, the two *Sylvie and Bruno* volumes disappointed the *Alice* enthusiasts of the period; and they have been largely honoured but unread by succeeding generations. There are of course the characteristically good things. 'What a comfort a Dictionary is', for instance, or 'It often runs in families, just as a love of pastry does'. The Gardener's song in all its variations had a nice touch of jingle madness which is catching:

> He thought he saw a Banker's Clerk
> Descending from a bus:
> He looked again and found it was
> A Hippopotamus:
> 'If this should stay to dine' he said
> 'There wo'n't be much for us.'

And this is what he had to tell his readers about the apostrophes in the last line: ' . . . critics have objected to certain innovations in spelling, such as "ca'n't", "wo'n't". In reply, I can only plead my firm conviction that the popular usage is *wrong*. As to "ca'n't", it will not be disputed that, in all *other* words ending in "n't", these letters are an abbreviation of "not"; and it is surely absurd to suppose that, in this solitary instance, "not" is represented by "'t"! In fact "can't" is the proper abbreviation for "can it", just as "is't" is for "is it". Again, in "Wo'n't", the first apostrophe is needed, because the word "would" is here abridged into "wo".'

This apostrophe fuss occurs in the second of the two explanatory and discursive prefaces which Carroll found necessary to write. Of

Opposite, frontispiece for *Sylvie and Bruno*. The book's length ('nearly as much as the two *Alice* books put together') made still more evident the absence of the *Alice* magic.

SWAIN SC

Harry Furniss

greater significance is a notion of human consciousness which he advanced:

I have supposed a Human being to be capable of various physical states, with varying degrees of consciousness, as follows:
(a) the ordinary state, with no consciousness of the presence of Fairies;
(b) the "eerie" state, in which, while conscious of actual surroundings, he is *also* conscious of the presence of Fairies;
(c) a form of trance, in which, while *un*conscious of actual surroundings, and apparently asleep, he (i.e. his immaterial essence) migrates to other scenes, in the actual world, or in Fairyland, and is conscious of the presence of Fairies.'

As a basis for his narrative this failed: as an explanation of the mind of the artist – his own not least – it is one of the most perceptive things he wrote.

It is sad too in that it emphasizes the nature of the failure of the *Sylvie and Bruno* books. He who was so passionately interested in knowledge, in absorbing and applying knowledge, simply knew too much. He knew the way into what he called Fairyland. While it is useful for us to have the benefit of his exploration, no writer should know that much. He knew too much and he tried too hard. Not even the most exquisite moments with the child friends could provide the threshold to creative reality, to Fairyland. He experienced what most poets, periodically or finally, consciously or unconsciously, experience – loss of creative nerve. *Sylvie and Bruno* did not come to life, though he put into it so much of himself and so much hope. He moralized, preached, joked, sang songs, prophesied about space, offered dissertations on fox-hunting, socialism, teetotalism. He added a strong pinch of snobbery, and the relentless phonetic baby talk of the boy-fairy Bruno: 'Flenchmen *never* can speak English so goodly as *us*!' or 'Had oo some of that funny stuff in oor hat *today*?'

'I am strongly of opinion,' he announced, 'that an author had far better *not* read any review of his books: the unfavourable ones are almost certain to make him cross, and the favourable ones conceited.'

For this reason, perhaps, it dawned on him rather tardily that the *Sylvie and Bruno* books were not commercially as successful as *Alice* continued to be. In 1894 he wrote to Macmillan's, 'Don't do any more *extra* advertising – it seems to be only throwing money away. I did not know the reviews had been unfavourable.'

The 1880s had not been the happiest period for him. He had known ill health for the first time, and applied himself to his medical books with hypochondriacal intensity. He had abandoned photography. He had given up his lectureship and taken on the Common Room chore. It is conjectured by some that Alice Liddell's marriage in

1880 cast a shadow over his life for a time, though this seems unlikely when he was cherishing so many other relationships.

During the last seven years of his life, in the 1890s, good health returned. He worked as hard as ever. He preached more. He wrote in a letter in August 1894: 'To say I am quite well "goes without saying" with me. In fact my life is so strangely free from all trial and trouble that I cannot doubt my own happiness is one of the talents entrusted to me to "occupy" with, till the Master shall return, by doing something to make other lives happy.'

He not only took exhaustingly long health walks, but acquired a Whiteley exerciser and allowed himself to get too thin. Though he withdrew from social life – he enjoyed a prodigious amount of it anyway – he continued to enjoy the triangle of pleasures afforded by Oxford, London and Eastbourne, together with dutiful attendance at the family home at Guildford. Within the spacious shelter of his Oxford rooms he kept up with the times, acquiring a fountain pen, out of which, recalled a child friend, 'the ink seemed to flow like black cream'.

While his search for knowledge and his exploration of mathematics went on relentlessly, demanding rigorous intellectual disciplines and

Beachy Head, a landscape familiar to Carroll. Till the end of his life he continued to take long country walks.

standards, he required merely entertainment in the arts. While he never significantly mentions the great painting of, say, the Renaissance, or even of Constable or Turner, he could be carried away by the narrative pieces at the Royal Academy – *More Free Than Welcome* by William Crawford ('a very sweet picture of a child sitting up in bed'), or Millais's *Boyhood of Sir Walter Raleigh* ('the cleverest thing there').

He explained his pleasure in light music: 'We do not feel called on to enjoy it to the utmost: we may take things as they come.' Of classical music he makes little mention until Bach came to be performed in Oxford in the 1870s: 'Bach's "Passion-Music" performed in the Cathedral to about 1200 people. I did not go. I think it is a pity churches be so used.'

His enthusiasm for the theatre – and for taking little girls to it – lasted till the end. On his last visit to a London theatre some six weeks before his death, he went to the Haymarket to see *The Little Minister*, 'a play I should like to see again and again'.

But it was the second part of his *Symbolic Logic* which occupied his waking thoughts when he developed bronchial trouble at Guildford in January 1898. At first he worried about his work on revision, then, as his breathing became laboured, he got one of his sisters to read aloud a hymn. Perhaps he lingered in the wind-swept boyhood fields of Daresbury and beneath the skylight where the workmen wrote their names outside his bedroom in the tall Rectory at Croft, where first 'twas brillig, before, at half-past two on 14 January, he died.

Opposite, Connie Gilchrist, child actor, friend of Carroll, and later Countess of Orkney, in Leighton's *The Music Lesson*. 'The most gloriously beautiful child that I ever saw,' Carroll took her to the Royal Academy in 1877, 'which she seemed to enjoy, particularly seeing Mr Leighton's picture of herself'.

Dying just short of this century, Lewis Carroll was on the outer edges of living memory when this book came to be written in the mid-1970s. So it was a bit of author's luck when Eric Norris, the Woolwich bookseller, casually mentioned having recently had tea at a Worthing guest-house with a lady who had actually met Lewis Carroll at Oxford. Here was one witness at least who had known my subject personally. Mrs Edith Bigg was well into her nineties, but wrote by return in a firm hand specifying a choice of times for an interview.

The guest-house was deep in afternoon sleep when, in a suitably hushed voice, I asked the lady who answered the door if Mrs Bigg could be seen. 'But I am Mrs Bigg!' declared this sprightly nonagenarian who calculated that she, then Edith Day, had been eight years old when she last went to tea at Christ Church with the author of *Alice* (a book which she, unlike many children, had even at that age already enjoyed). She was a little overawed by the famous, tall, gaunt yet lively clergyman then nearing the end of his life, but was soon captivated by his playing a phonograph, carefully closing the lid so as not to disturb students in adjoining rooms. The teatime conversation had been entertaining and rather flattering for a little girl of eight. Even in his last years he had retained his skill for communicating with the very young, supported always by a host of gadgets, toys and puzzles kept for the purpose – for he was nothing if not methodical.

So I first have to thank Mrs Bigg for her personal recollections, some Carroll letters, and her own engagingly agile demonstrations of the Carroll walk – like someone wading through grass against a strongish wind.

I thank Professor Morton N. Cohen, wise and resolute editor of the 98,721 items of Carroll correspondence, who has been accessible and generous; and Mr Derek Hudson, author of the really essential biography, *Lewis Carroll*, for his permission to make use of material. Members of the Lewis Carroll Society have not only been helpful over the written word, but quite fortuitously provided a realization of *Alice* at the bottom of my garden when their exhibition visited the Ranger's House before moving to Hatfield.

In the footsteps of Carroll I was assisted by the vicar of Daresbury, the birthplace; at Croft by the rector, Canon T.A. Littleton; at Christ Church, Oxford, by the assistant librarian, Mr H.J.R. Wing; and by Mr David Galer, director of the Towner Art Gallery at Eastbourne.

Greenwich 1975   JOHN PUDNEY

1832 27 January, born at Daresbury Parsonage, Cheshire.

1843 Family moves to Croft Rectory, Yorkshire.

1845 Produces *Useful and Instructive Poetry*, first of the family magazines.

1846 Enters Rugby School.

1851 January, comes into residence at Christ Church, Oxford. Death of his mother, Frances Jane Dodgson. November, awarded the Boulter Scholarship.

1852 December, obtains a First in Maths Moderations. 24 December, nominated to a Studentship (Fellowship) at Christ Church, on Dr Pusey's recommendation.

1854 Summer reading-party at Whitby, Yorkshire. First works published, in the *Oxonian Advertiser* and the *Whitby Gazette* ('The Lady of the Ladle'). October, obtains a First in the Final Mathematical School. December, becomes a Bachelor of Arts.

1855 February, made 'Master of the House' to celebrate the arrival of the new dean, Dr H. G. Liddell. May, awarded the Bostock Scholarship. Contributes to the *Comic Times*. Writes the first verse of 'Jabberwocky' ('Twas bryllyg ...') in a serapbook. September, his interest in photography is aroused by his uncle, Skeffington Lutwidge. Writes 'Photographer Extraordinary'. Becomes a keen London theatre-goer.

1856 Contributes to *The Train* (successor to the *Comic Times*). March, the pen-name of 'Lewis Carroll' first appears (in *The Train*). 18 March, orders a complete set of photographic apparatus. June, takes his first successful photographs.

1857 Becomes a Master of Arts. Meets Holman Hunt, Ruskin. Summer, visits and photographs Tennyson and family at Coniston, Lake District. November, writes 'Hiawatha's Photographing'.

1858 February, exhibits at the Photographic Society of London's fifth exhibition.

1859 April, visits Tennyson at Farringford, Isle of Wight.

1860 First book published: *A Syllabus of Plane Algebraical Geometry*. 'A Photographer's Day Out' appears in the *South Shields Amateur Magazine*.

1861 Contributes to *College Rhymes*. December, ordained deacon by Samuel Wilberforce, Bishop of Oxford.

1862 4 July, tells the story of *Alice* during a boat trip to Godstow with the Liddell children. 13 November, begins to write down *Alice's Adventures Under Ground* for Alice Liddell.

1863 February, finishes *Alice's Adventures Under Ground*. Meets D. G. and Christina Rossetti.

1864 Sends the specially illustrated MS of *Alice* to Alice Liddell. Expands original MS and retitles it *Alice's Adventures in Wonderland*. April, final arrangements for publication are settled with Tenniel, the illustrator, and Macmillan, the publisher. Meets Millais and family, Arthur Hughes, etc.

1865 May, first specimen volume of *Alice's Adventures in Wonderland* sent to Carroll.

1866 *Condensation of Determinants* published. Meets the novelist Charlotte M. Yonge.

1867 *An Elementary Treatise on Determinants*. July–September, travels to Russia with Dr H. Liddon. 'Bruno's Revenge' (the nucleus of *Sylvie and Bruno*) appears in *Aunt Judy's Magazine*.

1868 June, Carroll's father dies. He acquires 'The Chestnuts', Guildford, for his sisters and arranges the family's move. August, Alice Raikes becomes the inspiration for *Through the Looking-Glass*. October, moves into new rooms in Tom Quad, Christ Church.

1869 *Phantasmagoria* published.

1870 Meets the new Chancellor, Lord Salisbury, and later his family and children, Lady Maud and Lady Gwendolen Cecil.

1871 January, *Through the Looking-Glass* completed. December, *Through the Looking-Glass* published.

1872 Becomes involved in University controversies with the anonymous publication of an anti-Liddell pamphlet, *The New Belfry of Christ Church, Oxford*. Makes use of the photographic 'glass-house' built for him over his rooms in Tom Quad.

1873 Begins telling *Sylvie and Bruno* stories to Maud and Gwendolen Cecil at Hatfield House.

1874 July, the last line of *Snark* comes into his head during a Guildford walk.

1875 Summer, at Sandown, Isle of Wight, works on *Snark*. He is encouraged by his meeting with a new child friend, Gertrude Chataway, to whom he dedicates it.

1876 March, publication of *The Hunting of the Snark*. Suggests (and thus invents) the idea of 'dust-covers' or jackets for books. First dramatic presentation of *Alice* stories.

1877 Summer, first of his regular visits to Eastbourne, continued till his death.

1878 *Word-Links* published, a collection of puzzles and word-games.

1879 *Euclid and his Modern Rivals.*

1880 Takes a cut of £100 (one-third) in his salary as mathematics lecturer. July, gives up photography. September, death of Aunt Lucy Lutwidge. Marriage of Alice Liddell to Reginald Hargreaves.

1881 Resigns his mathematics lectureship at Christ Church. Publishes *Euclid, Books I and II.*

1882 Takes on the job of Curator of the Senior Common Room at Christ Church.

1883 *Rhyme? and Reason?*

1885 *A Tangled Tale.*

1886 Publishes facsimile of *Alice's Adventures Under Ground. Alice in Wonderland* produced at the Prince of Wales Theatre, London.

1887 *The Game of Logic.* Writes to the *St James's Gazette* defending the employment of children in theatres.

1888 *Curiosa Mathematica, Part I.*

1889 December, *Sylvie and Bruno* published with a dedicatory acrostic to his child friend Isa Bowman.

1890 Publication of *The Nursery Alice* for very young children, and *Circular Billiards.* Invents 'The Wonderland Postage-Stamp Case'.

1892 Resigns as Curator of the Senior Common Room.

1893 *Sylvie and Bruno Concluded. Curiosa Mathematica, II (Pillow Problems).*

1896 *Symbolic Logic, Part I.*

1898 14 January, dies at Guildford.

SELECT BIBLIOGRAPHY

Bowman, Isa, *The Story of Lewis Carroll*, London, 1899; New York, 1972 (as *Lewis Carroll as I knew him*).

Carroll, Lewis, *Alice's Adventures Under Ground*, London, 1886; New York, 1965.

— *The Complete Works of Lewis Carroll*, introduced by Alexander Woollcott, New York, 1937; London, 1939.

Collingwood, Stuart Dodgson (ed.), *The Lewis Carroll Picture Book*, London, 1899; New York, 1961 (as *The Unknown Lewis Carroll*).

— *The Life and Letters of Lewis Carroll*, London, 1898; Detroit, MI, 1967.

De la Mare, Walter, *Lewis Carroll*, London, 1930; New York, 1972.

Gardner, Martin (ed.), *The Annotated Alice*, New York, 1960; Harmondsworth, 1965.

— *The Annotated Snark*, New York, 1962; Harmondsworth, 1967.

Gernsheim, Helmut, *Lewis Carroll, Photographer*, London, 1949; New York, 1969.

Green, Roger Lancelyn (ed.), *The Diaries of Lewis Carroll*, two vols, London, 1953.

Hatch, Evelyn M. (ed.), *A Selection from the Letters of Lewis Carroll to his Child-Friends*, London, 1933; Folcroft PA, 1973.

Hudson, Derek, *Lewis Carroll*, London, 1954; Philadelphia PA, 1954.

McDermott, John Francis (ed.), *The Russian Journal, etc.*, New York, 1935.

Phillips, Robert (ed.), *Aspects of Alice*, New York, 1971; London, 1972; Harmondsworth, 1974.

Taylor, Alexander L., *The White Knight*, Edinburgh, 1952; Philadelphia PA, 1973.

Williams, Sidney H. and Falconer Madan, *A Handbook of the Literature of the Rev. C.L. Dodgson*, London, 1931.

LIST OF ILLUSTRATIONS

Wilfred Dodgson; photograph by Lewis Carroll. Morris L. Parrish collection. Princeton University Library

44 Magdalen College barge; nineteenth-century photograph. Bodleian Library, Oxford

45 View of Whitby harbour; photograph by Frank Sutcliffe. Sutcliffe Gallery, Whitby

48 Drawing by Lewis Carroll for *The Three Voices*, 1856

49 Queen Catherine's Dream: scene from Shakespeare's *Henry VIII*; illustration from *Illustrated London News*, 1855. Raymond Mander and Joe Mitchenson Theatre Collection

51 Dean Liddell; photograph by Hills and Saunders. Graham Ovenden collection

52 Caricature of Lewis Carroll by himself. *Life and Letters of Lewis Carroll*, 1898

Undergraduates of the 1860s; cartoon by Sidney Prior Hall (1842–1922). Christ Church library

53 Quintin F. Twiss as the Artful Dodger; photograph by Lewis Carroll, 1858. Morris L. Parrish collection, Princeton University Library

54 Illustration by A.B. Frost from 'Hiawatha's Photographing' in *Rhyme? and Reason?* by Lewis Carroll, 1883

Lewis Carroll with Greville, Mary, Irene and Grace, children of George MacDonald.

55 Tom Taylor; photograph by Lewis Carroll, 1863. Gernsheim collection, University of Texas

56 Photographer processing a plate; woodcut by A. Jahandiez

57 Tom Quad, Christ Church; late nineteenth-century photograph. Christ Church library

Lewis Carroll's study at Christ Church; Dodgson family collection, Muniment Room, Guildford

61 Labyrinth drawn by Lewis Carroll for Georgina Watson

62 Lord Tennyson; photograph by Lewis Carroll, 1857. Gernsheim collection, University of Texas

Hallam Tennyson; photograph by Lewis Carroll, 1857. Graham Ovenden collection

63 Railway station, Ventnor, Isle of Wight. H. Chapman collection

66 Crown Prince Frederick of Denmark; photograph by Lewis Carroll, 1863. Gernsheim collection, University of Texas

John Everett Millais, his wife and daughters Effie and Mary; photograph by Lewis Carroll, 1865. Gernsheim collection, University of Texas

The Misses Lutwidge playing chess; photograph by Lewis Carroll *c.* 1858. Gernsheim collection, University of Texas

67 'Coates'; photograph by Lewis Carroll, 1857. Gernsheim collection, University of Texas

68 Lewis Carroll. Dodgson family collection, Muniment Room, Guildford

69 Alice and caterpillar; illustration by Lewis Carroll in *Alice's Adventures Under Ground*, 1864. British Library, London

70 Alice Liddell; photograph by Lewis Carroll, 1870. Reproduced from *The Lewis Carroll Picture Book*, 1899

Alice Liddell; photograph by Julia Margaret Cameron, 1872. National Portrait Gallery, London

73 'The Wonderland Postage-Stamp Case', 1889. Courtesy Messrs. B. Rota, London

74 Alice; drawings by Lewis Carroll on pages 6 and 17 of MS *Alice's Adventures Under Ground*, 1864. British Library, London

75 Page 62 from MS, *Alice's Adventures Under Ground*, 1864. British Library, London

76 Grotesque Old Woman, previously called *The Ugly Duchess*, ascribed to Quinten Massys (1465–1530). National Gallery, London

The Duchess and Alice; John Tenniel's illustration in *Alice in Wonderland*, 1865

77 Sir John Tenniel; photograph British Museum

Mary Hilton Badcock; photograph from *Handbook of the Literature of the Rev. C.L. Dodgson*, Williams and Madan, 1931

The White Knight and Alice; frontispiece by J. Tenniel, *Through the Looking-Glass*, 1871

78 The public leaving after the performance of *Little King Pippin* at Drury Lane; *Illustrated London News*, 6 January 1866

82 Letter by mirror writing from Lewis Carroll to Edith Ball, 1893

83 The Jabberwock; illustration by J. Tenniel in *Through the Looking-Glass*, 1871

85 'To pursue it with forks and hope'; illustration by Henry Holiday in *The Hunting of the Snark*, 1876

86 Henry Holiday in his studio; photograph from *Life and Letters of Lewis Carroll*, 1898

87 The Boojum; suppressed drawing by Henry Holiday shown at the Lewis Carroll exhibition of 1932 and reproduced in *Illustrated London News*, 9 July 1932

INDEX

Page numbers in italics indicate illustrations